James Parish Stelle

The American Watchmaker and Jeweler

James Parish Stelle

The American Watchmaker and Jeweler

ISBN/EAN: 9783337021511

Printed in Europe, USA, Canada, Australia, Japan

Cover: Foto ©Andreas Hilbeck / pixelio.de

More available books at **www.hansebooks.com**

In Press.—To be ready in October, 1873.

HAIR ORNAMENTS

FOR

JEWELRY AND SOUVENIRS:

A GUIDE FOR

A tasteful recreation for leisure hours, and a lucrative
employment for Jewelers and others.

With over 80 Illustrative Engravings.

Price 50 cents. For sale by all booksellers, or mailed,
post-paid, on receipt of price, fifty cents, by

JESSE HANEY & CO.,

No. 119 Nassau-st., New York.

THE

AMERICAN WATCHMAKER

AND

JEWELER,

A FULL AND COMPREHENSIVE EXPOSITION

OF ALL THE

𝕷atest and most 𝕬pproved 𝕾ecrets of the 𝕮rade

EMBRACING

WATCH AND CLOCK CLEANING AND REPAIRING, TEMPERING
IN ALL ITS GRADES, MAKING TOOLS, COMPOUND-
ING METALS, SOLDERING. PLATING, ETC.,

WITH A SERIES OF PLAIN INSTRUCTIONS FOR BEGINNERS.

ALSO,

DIRECTIONS BY WHICH THOSE NOT FINDING IT CONVE-
NIENT TO PATRONIZE A HOROLOGIST MAY KEEP
THEIR CLOCKS IN ORDER.

BY J. PARISH STELLE,
A PRACTICAL WATCHMAKER.

New York:
JESSE HANEY & CO., PUBLISHERS,
119 NASSAU STREET.

HANEY'S TRADE MANUALS.

PUBLISHERS' NOTICE.

THE AMERICAN WATCHMAKER AND JEWELER is the initial issue of a series of "TRADE MANUALS" which we propose publishing as fast as they can be properly prepared. The value of books treating of the processes, manipulations and discoveries of the different trades and professions is recognized by every intelligent man. While no book can pretend to be a substitute for experience and natural ability, in the prosecution of any industry, there is unquestionably much information that can be told in a few moments, which might require years to arrive at by individual experiments. A guide of this kind should embrace the combined results of all discoveries and improvements in the art of which it treats, so as to keep pace with the progress constantly taking place.

There are many good books relating to the different trades, and we consider that a liberal expenditure for such would prove profitable to every artisan. Such books are necessarilly higher priced than common works. The main objection to most of them is that they contain much unimportant matter which swells them in both size and price, at the same time that it confuses the reader. We shall attempt to obviate this objection in HANEY'S TRADE MANUALS by giving in concise form all the really valuable information attainable on the subjects treated. Great care will be taken to make them reliable in every respect, and of real assistance to the reader. They will be almost wholly original, written by practical and experienced men. In order that they may have a large and general circulation, and be within reach of every person engaged in the occupation they treat of, HANEY'S TRADE MANUALS will be sold at the lowest prices, considering the original cost of preparation, manufacture of books, and the extent of the demand. Those which, from the limited extent of any trade, necessarilly have but a small circulation, must of course be charged somewhat higher than those appertaining to more extensive interests. We shall, however, in every case content ourselves with a moderate and reasonable profit in our investment

PREFACE.

⸺∘⊶⊷∘⸺

I DO not expect all watchmakers to praise me for having presented this exposition of the " secrets of the trade," no more than the physician who produces a work adapted to domestic practice could reasonably expect a blessing from every member of the medical profession. It is all the same to me. I did not write it for praise ; nor did I write it under the conviction that I was doing anything deserving of blame. I expect to *be* blamed, however, and to have hard things said of me by a few who either feel that they know enough already to make out with, and would rather not have the secrets imparted to others lest they in consequence should come in for a share in the success ; or who are making a good thing of it by selling " The Latest and Most Improved Processes " to the less fortunate, at the moderate price of from three to forty dollars each. I know just about what they will say of me : that I shall leave between them and their own consciences. I know, too, about how they will argue with a view to creating a foundation for blame : of that I may speak a word or two. They will intimate that there are too many " botches" in the business already, and that a work of this character is only calculated to augment their number.

At first thought this thing may appear reasonable enough, but a sober second reflection will convince any reasonable person of its inability to hold good. That there are " botches," and sad ones, following the vocation I must admit ; and what is still worse, many of them are men who have enjoyed excellent opportunities for gaining information. As a general thing, a lack of capacity rather than information has made them " botches," and this very custom of husbanding the " secrets of the trade " from the public is what enables them to curse the communities in which they are located, by holding positions which would otherwise be filled by better men.   So long as horological information can only be obtained at a high price, a large number of unqualified persons, who happen to be financially favored, will buy it, and "botches" must be the result, of course. But not so when we place it within the reach of all.   Men qualified for the business will then take hold of it, and such as are now imposing upon the people, simply because they happen to possess a few secrets too costly to be generally known, will find themselves under the necessity of falling back.   France is said to be blessed with the most skillful watchmakers in the world, and the reason is plain—she is the only nation whose authors have attempted to produce a series of cheap and reliable books on the science of horology.

This is my argument.   It was what prompted me to write this book ; and though I might produce other arguments in favor of the move, I think it is enough.

I shall not speak of the character or claims of the AMERICAN WATCHMAKER AND JEWELER, preferring that the book should show for itself.   A knowledge of the fact that superior opportunities for acquiring the latest and best information touching this, my favorite subject, have presented themselves and been eagerly embraced by me, both in Europe and America, emboldens me to send forth the work without a single misgiving.

THE AUTHOR.

CONTENTS.

ON PLATING.

MISCELLANEOUS RECIPES.

THE AMERICAN

WATCHMAKER AND JEWELER.

CHAPTER I.

INTRODUCTION.

THE American watchmaker, so called, is not usually a
manufacturer of watches, or even parts of watches, but
simply an artist whose business it is to repair and keep
watches in order. He is generally a man of rare mechanical genius, capable of turning his hand to almost anything,
hence he is not unfrequently, especially in the country, also
a clockmaker—in the same sense—a jeweler, and a repairer
of musical instruments. In short the good watchmaker is
almost invariably, if he is disposed to let himself out, a
Jack-of-all-trades. He must possess a degree of ingenuity
sufficient to qualify him for almost any mechanical perform-
ance without the benefit of a previous apprenticeship, or he
cannot be a successful watchmaker, for it is a business in
which there is no regular routine, as in other trades. Any
industrious person, though endowed with nothing above an
ordinary capacity, may, in obedience to a long series of instructions combined with practice, make a master carpenter,
blacksmith or wheelwright of himself, but not a watchmaker.
The watchmaker whose skill is to render him deserving of
the application, must be blessed with a natural gift above
the generality. Like the painter, the sculptor or the poet,
he must be born to the calling. Not only must he be what

is termed a natural mechanic, but a philosopher as well, possessed of a good reasoning power of his own; for instances are sure to occur, and often, in which he will be called upon to ferret out causes and effects never met with or thought of by his instructions.

I throw in these hints, not with a view to the discouragement of any, but in the hope that they may be of benefit to some who are thinking of becoming watchmakers. If the true element is in them it has given evidence of the fact, and they may go ahead with confidence of success; if not, they had better abandon the idea at once and turn attention to something else; bearing in mind that all were not made for the same vocation, and that he who would not make a useful watchmaker, might more than succeed at some other calling. True, a person might get along at the business without these extra qualifications named, but there would be no chances for him to excel, and unless one could be an excellent watchmaker he had far better be no watchmaker at all. Unfortunately for us, and for them, there are already too many second and third class workmen of the kind in America.

Parents who contemplate putting their children to trades should bear in mind the important truths on which I have just been treating. The best years of a boy's life may be literally wasted in the acquirement of a vocation for which he has no natural qualifications.

To within a few years back horology was at a low ebb in the United States. It is beginning to look up now, however, with excellent prospects for a glorious future. I am of the opinion that the day is not far distant when she will make not only all her own time-pieces, but will furnish a very large proportion of those used in other parts of the world. This conclusion I base upon what she has done and is doing already. It is truly astonishing when we take into consideration the fact that the business was a stranger to her shores up to the beginning of the nineteenth century.

The first attempt at producing machines on American soil for the measurement of time was made by Eli Terry of Plymouth Hollow, Conn., A. D. 1800, in the manufacture of the old fashioned wooden clocks. He went into the business on an exceedingly small scale at first, doing, I think, all the work himself, and acting as his own salesman and traveling agent. He would finish two or three clocks, it is said, and swinging them upon the back of a horse, would strike out into the country and peddle till the last one was sold; then, but not till then, he would return to his home and engage in the manufacture of a new cargo.

The excellence of Mr. Terry's clocks, and their cheapness when compared to that of the imported article, soon caused his business to grow until the erection of a large establishment became necessary. This continued in successful operation until Mr. Terry's death a few years ago.

When it became known that the Plymouth Hollow clock factory was a paying institution, other establishments sprung up to rival it. Great improvements were made both in the materials worked and the manner of working them. Indeed, so rapid was the progress made that only a few brief years passed ere America was famed abroad for producing the best clocks in the world, and large exportations were constantly being made.

An establishment for the manufacture of watches went into operation at Worcester, Mass., in 1812, but soon failed. In 1830, another was started at Hartford, Conn., but after turning out near one thousand watches it too went down, and the hope of competing successfully with English work seemed to die out for the present.

In 1850, Mr. A. L. Dennison of Maine suggested the idea of manufacturing a watch entire in one establishment, by properly constructed machinery—a thing not yet thought of in Europe. Others took with the idea and soon joined him in the erection of a manufactory at Roxbury, Mass.

The plan worked to the satisfaction of all concerned, but the site was found to be unsuitable on account of the dust; consequently, in 1854, the concern was removed to Waltham, in the same state, where it is still (1868) in successful operation, turning out the celebrated "American Watches" in large numbers. It is known as "The American Watch Company of Waltham, Mass.," and its watches have acquired a good reputation.

A second watch manufactory on Mr. Dennison's plan, was established at Nashua, New Hampshire, but want of capital soon caused it to fail, and the American Watch

Company bought its machinery. A third is now in operation at Elgin, Illinois, near Chicago, under style of "The National Watch Company." It was established in 1867, and its productions have a very excellent reputation.

———o◦○◦○○———

CHAPTER II.

ON WATCH CLEANING.

It is hardly necessary to say that great caution must be observed in taking the watch down—that is, in separating its parts. If you are new at the business think before you act, and then act slowly. Take off the hands carefully so as not to bend the slender pivots upon which they work; this will be the first step. Second—loosen and lift the movement from the case. Third—remove the dial and dial wheels. Fourth—let down the main-spring by placing your bench key upon the arbor, or "winding post," and turning as though you were going to wind the watch until the click rests lightly upon the ratchet; then with your screw-driver press the point of the click away from the teeth, and ease down the spring. Fifth—draw the screws (or pins) and remove the bridges of the train, or the upper plate, as the case may be. Sixth—take out the balance. Great care must be observed in this or you will injure the hair-spring. The stud or little square post into which the hair-spring is fastened may be removed from the bridge or plate of most modern watches, without unkeying the spring, by slipping a thin instrument, as the edge of a knife blade, under the corner of it and prizing upward. This will save you a considerable amount of trouble, as you will not have the hair spring to adjust when you reset the balance.

If the watch upon which you propose to work has an upper plate, as an American or an English lever for instance, loosen the lever before you have entirely separated the plates, otherwise it will hang and most likely be broken.

Having the machine now down, brush the dust from its

different parts and subject them to a careful examination
with your eye-glass. Assure yourself that the teeth of the
wheels and leaves of the pinions are all perfect and smooth ;
that the pivots are all straight, round and highly polished ;
that the holes through which they are to work, are not too
large, and have not become oval in shape ; that every jewel
is smooth and perfectly sound ; and that none of them are
loose in their settings. See, also, that the escapement is not
too deep or too shallow ; that the lever or cylinder is perfect ; that all the wheels have sufficient play to avoid friction, but not enough to derange their coming together properly ; that none of them work against the pillar-plate ; that
the balance turns horizontally and does not rub ; that the
hair-spring is not bent or wrongly set so that the coils rub on
each other, on the plate or on the balance ; in short, that
everything about the whole movement is just as reason
would teach you it should be. If you find it otherwise, proceed to repair in accordance with a carefully weighed judg-
ment, and the processes given in next chapter, after which
clean—if not, the watch only needs to be cleaned, and therefore you may go ahead with your work at once.

TO CLEAN.

Many watchmakers wet the pillar plates and bridges with
saliva, and then dipping the brush into pulverized chalk or
Spanish whiting, rub vigorously until they appear bright.
This is not a good plan, as it tends to remove the plating
and roughen the parts, and the chalk gets into the holes and
damages them, or sticks around the edges of the wheel-beds.
The best process is to simply blow your breath upon the
plate or bridge to be cleaned, and then to use your brush
with a little prepared chalk—(See recipe for preparing it.)
The wheels and bridges should be held between the thumb
and finger in a piece of soft paper while undergoing the process ; otherwise the oil from the skin will prevent their becoming clean. The pinions may be cleaned by sinking them
several times into a piece of pith, and the holes by turning
a nicely shaped piece of pivot wood into them, first dry and
afterwards oiled a very little with watch oil. When the
holes pass through jewels you must work gently to avoid
breaking them.

The oiling above named is all the watch will need. A great fault with many watchmakers lies in their use of too much oil.

THE " CHEMICAL PROCESS."

Some watchmakers employ what they call the " Chemical Process" to clean and remove discolorations from watch movements.   It is as follows :—

Remove the screws and other steel parts ; then dampen with a solution of oxalic acid and water.   Let it remain a few moments, after which immerse in a solution made of one-fourth pound cyanuret potassa to one gallon rain water. Let remain about five minutes, and then rinse well with clean water, after which you may dry in sawdust, or with a brush and prepared chalk, as suits your convenience.   This gives the work an excellent appearance, but I cannot say that it makes it any better than does the old process.

TO PREPARE CHALK FOR CLEANING.

Pulverize your chalk thoroughly, and then mix it with clear rain water in the proportion of two pounds to the gallon.   Stir well and then let stand about two minutes. In this time the gritty matter will have settled to the bottom. Pour the water into another vessel, slowly so as not to stir up the settlings.   Let stand until entirely settled, and then pour off as before.   The settlings in the second vessel will be your prepared chalk, ready for use as soon as dried.

Spanish whiting treated in the same way makes a very good cleaning or polishing powder.   Some operatives add a little jeweler's rouge, and I think it is an improvement ; it gives the powder a nice color at least, and therefore adds to its importance in the eyes of the uninitiated.   In cases where a sharper polishing powder is required, it may be prepared in the same way from rotten stone.

PIVOT WOOD.

Watchmakers usually buy this article of watch-material dealers.   A small shrub known as Indian arrow-wood, to be met with in the northern and western states, makes an excellent pivot wood.   It must be cut when the sap is down, and split into quarters so as to throw the pith outside of the rod.

PITH FOR CLEANING.

The stalk of the common mullen—*verbascum thapsus*—affords the best pith for cleaning pinions that I have ever yet tried.   It may be found in old fields and by-places all over the country.   Winter, when the stalk is dry, is the time to gather it.   Some workmen use cork instead of pith, but it is not so good and far less safe.

CHAPTER III.

ON WATCH REPAIRING.

I SHALL not attempt to describe, and to prescribe for, every species of defect that has been known to occur in a watch, for two reasons : The first is, that it would make a work far too large to come within the scope of my present plans, or to be useful ; and the second, that many of the defects constantly to be met with are of a character so simple, and so plain, that any person with ordinary ingenuity will be able to note them at once and apply the remedy.   Such, for instance, as putting in a main-spring, a hair-spring, or a jewel; a mere glance at the machine will be sufficient to satisfy the proposed operative with regard to the steps necessary to be taken, even though he may have never before seen the inside of a watch.

With a view, then, to giving my reader the largest possible amount of useful information for his money, I shall proceed at once to offer such modes employed in watch repairing as he could not easily acquire himself—in short, to present in the briefest possible manner a complete exposition of those processes in use, known as " The Secrets of the Trade."   Once they are mastered, he will find it no longer a difficult matter to carry on the watch-repairing business with credit and success; provided, of course, he possesses a reasonable amount of ingenuity and patience.

TO PIVOT.

When you find a pivot broken, you will hardly be at a loss to understand that the easiest mode of repairing the damage is to drill into the end of the pinion or staff, as the case may be, and having inserted a new pivot, turn it down to the proper proportions. This is by no means a difficult thing when the piece to be drilled is not too hard, or when the temper may be slightly drawn without injury to the other parts of the article. It will be difficult, however, in cases where you find it necessary.

TO DRILL INTO HARDENED STEEL.

For this purpose make your drill oval in form, instead of in the usual shape, and temper as hard as it will bear without crumbling. Roughen the surface of the object into which you desire to drill with a little diluted nitric acid. Start your drill, and to prevent it from becoming heated use spirits of turpentine instead of oil. Some workmen use kerosene with gum camphor dissolved in it instead of turpentine.

When your drill begins to run smooth in consequence of the bottom of the holes becoming burnished, clean out the turpentine or kerosene and roughen again with acid; then proceed as before.

You will find this a somewhat tedious business, but with a little patient application you will finally be able to accomplish your object. It is the only mode for drilling into highly tempered steel that will work with any degree of certainty.

TO TELL WHEN THE LEVER IS OF PROPER LENGTH.

You may readily learn whether or not a lever is of proper length, by measuring from the guard point to the pallet staff, and then comparing with the roller or ruby-pin table; the diameter of the table should always be just half the length measured on the lever. The rule will work both ways, and may be useful in cases when a new ruby-pin table has to be supplied.

TO LENGTHEN LEVERS OF ANCHOR ESCAPEMENTS.

Some do this by drawing the temper of the lever between the pallets and the fork and forging it out to the proper length ; others by soldering a piece the required thickness against the guard point just back of the fork.

There is a new process advertised by dealers in the "Secrets of the Trade"—price three dollars—as " The best and quickest means of bringing the point of the lever close to the roller, without hammering the point, soldering a piece on or stretching the lever." It is as follows :—

Cut across with a screw-head file, just back of the fork, as deeply as you can with safety. The thin point thus left standing to itself you will bend gently forward to the proper position. This is all that will be required. In the event you break the little point in your efforts to bend it—a thing not likely to happen—you can file down level, drill a hole and insert a pin American lever style.

TO CHANGE DEPTH OF LEVER ESCAPEMENT.

If you are operating on a fine watch the best plan is to put a new staff into the lever, cutting its pivots a little to one side—just as far as you desire to change the escapement. Common watches will not, of course, justify so much trouble. The usual process in their case is to knock out the staff, and with a small file cut the hole oblong in a direction opposite to that in which you desire to move your pallets ; then replace the staff, wedge it to the required position, and secure by soft soldering.

In instances where the staff is put in with a screw you will have to proceed differently. Take out the staff, prize the pallets from the lever, file the pin holes to slant in the direction you would move the pallets, without changing their size on the other side of the lever. Connect the pieces as they were before, and with the lever resting on some solid substance you may strike lightly with your hammer until the bending of the pins will allow the pallets to pass into position.

TO TELL WHEN THE LEVER PALLETS ARE OF PROPER SIZE.

The clear space between the pallets should correspond .

with the outside measure, on the points, of three teeth of
the scape wheel. The usual mode of measuring for new
pallets is to set the wheel as close as possible to free itself
when in motion. You can arrange it in your depthing tool,
after which a measurement between the pivot holes of the
two pieces, on the pillar plate, will show you exactly what
s required.

TO PUT TEETH INTO WHEELS

Most watchmakers solder or dovetail their teeth in, but
there is a new mode which I consider far better, and I know
it is easier: Make a hole through the plate of the wheel
immediately below the point from which the tooth has been
broken. Let its diameter be a little greater than the width
of a tooth. Next, with your tooth-saw cut down where the
tooth should stand till you come into the hole. You then
dress out with a head upon it, a piece of brass wire, till it
fits nicely into the cut of the saw, with its head in the hole.
With a fine graver you then cut a crease into the wheel-
plate above and below, on either side of the newly-fitted
wire; after which, with your hammer, you cautiously spread
the face of the wire until it fills the creases, and is securely
clinched or riveted into the wheel. This makes a strong
job, and one that dresses up to look as well as any other.

TO WEAKEN THE HAIR-SPRING.

This is often effected by grinding the spring down. You
remove the spring from the collet, and place it upon a piece
of pivot wood cut to fit the centre coil. A piece of soft
steel wire, flattened so as to pass freely between the coils,
and armed with a little pulverized oil-stone and oil, will
serve as your grinder, and with it you may soon reduce the
strength of the spring. Your operations will, of course, be
confined to the centre coil, for no other part of the spring
will rest sufficiently against the wood to enable you to grind
it, but this will generally suffice. The effect will be more
rapid than one would suppose, therefore it will stand you in
hand to be careful or you may get the spring too weak before
you suspect it.
Another and perhaps later process is as follows : Fit the

collet, without removing the spring, upon a stick of pivot-wood, and having prepared a little diluted nitric acid in a watch-glass, plunge the centre coils into it, keeping the other parts of the spring from contact by holding it in the shape of an inverted hoop skirt, with your tweezers. Expose it a few seconds, governing the time of course by the degree of effect desired, and then rinse off, first with clean water, and afterwards with alcohol. Dry in the sun or with tissue paper.

TO PREVENT A CHAIN FROM RUNNING OFF THE FUSEE.

In the first place you must look after and ascertain the cause of the difficulty. If it results from the chain's being too large, the only remedy is a new chain. If it is not too large, and yet runs off without any apparent cause, change it end for end—that will generally make it go all right. In cases where the channel in the fusee has been damaged, and is rough, you will be under the necessity of dressing it over with a file the proper size and shape. Sometimes you find the chain naturally inclined to work away from the body of the fusee. The best way to remedy a difficulty of this kind is to file off a very little from the outer lower edge of the chain the entire length—this, as you can see, will incline it to work on instead of off. Some workmen, when they have a bad case, and a common watch, change the standing of the fusee so as to cause the winding end of its arbor to incline a little from the barrel. This, of course, cannot do otherwise than make the chain run to its place.

TO PUT WATCHES IN BEAT.

If a cylinder escapement, or a detached lever, put the balance into position, then turn the regulator so that it will point directly to the pivot-hole of the pallet staff if a lever, or of the scape-wheel if a cylinder. Then lift out the balance with its bridge or clock, turn it over and set the ruby pin directly in line with the regulator, or the square cut of the cylinder at right angles with it. Your watch will then be in perfect beat.

In case of an American or an English lever, when the regulator is placed upon the plate, you will have to proceed

differently.   Fix the balance into its place, cut off the connection of the train, if the mainspring is not entirely down,
by slipping a fine broach into one of the wheels, then look
between the plates and ascertain how the lever stands.   If
the end farthest from the balance is equi-distant between
the two brass pins it is all right—if not, change the hair-
spring till it becomes so.   .

If dealing with a duplex watch, you must see that the
roller notch, when the balance is at rest, is exactly between
the locking tooth and the line of centres—that is, a line drawn
from the centre of the roller to the centre of the scape-
wheel.   The balance must start from its rest and move
through an arc of about ten degrees before bringing the
locking tooth into action.

TO TIGHTEN A COMMON-PINION ON THE CENTRE ARBOR.

The most common way is to put a hair into the cannon
and force it down upon the arbor, but this is objectionable
from the fact that it sets the pinion just the width of the
hair to one side.   Another way is to twist the arbor lightly
into a pair of cutting plyers, raising a thread or burr upon
it.   I could not recommend this mode as there is too much
danger of bending the arbor in the operation.   I generally
roll the arbor between two files, letting the square part be to
one side of them, of course.   A very slight roll between
two files will generally tighten the cannon, and there can
be no danger of bending the arbor or setting the pinions to
one side.

TO TIGHTEN A RUBY PIN.

Set the ruby pin in asphaltum varnish.   It will become
hard in a few minutes, and be much firmer and better than
gum shellac, as generally used.

CHAPTER IV.

ON MENDING WATCH TRAINS.

WHEN a wheel or a pinion is wanting in the train of a watch, it is usual to say the train is broken; and the act of supplying that wheel or pinion is generally termed mending the train. This, according to the old plan of working involved no small amount of labor, in the way of calculations, to get the proper size of the new piece. A person was under the necessity of being a good algebra scholar to do it. The recent, or I might say the American system—for European watchmakers still hold to their old ways—makes it much easier. A few simple tables have been gotten up by which any person who knows how to count and to measure may select the piece he wants in a few minutes.

TO DETERMINE THE REQUIRED DIAMETER OF A PINION.

For size of Pinion with	Measures on Wheel.	Character of Measure.
4 leaves, ...	2 teeth,......	Very full from out to out.
5 leaves, ...	3 teeth,......	Exactly from centre to centre.
6 leaves, ...	3 teeth,......	Full from centre to centre.
7 leaves, ...	3 teeth,......	Scant from out to out.
8 leaves, ...	4 teeth,......	Scant from centre to centre.
9 leaves, ...	4 teeth,......	Full from out to out.
10 leaves, ...	4 teeth,......	Exactly from out to out.
12 leaves	5 teeth,......	Exactly from centre to centre.
14 leaves, . .	6 teeth,......	Scant from centre to centre.
15 leaves.....	6 teeth,......	Scant from out to out.
17 leaves, ...	7 teeth,......	Full from centre to centre.

TABLES OF NON-SECOND WATCH TRAINS.

Centre wheel.	3d Wheel and Pinion.		4th Wheel and Pinion.			Scape Wheel and Pinion.		Beats per minute.	Character of trains.
No. of teeth in wheel.	Teeth in wheel.	Leaves in pin.	Teeth in wheel.	Leaves in l'in.	Seconds in revolutions	Teeth in wheel.	Leaves in pin.	No. of beats.	
66	63	6	63	6	31	7	6	283 scant	Trains for seven teeth in scape wheel.
66	64	6	63	6	31	7	6	287 full	
66	64	6	64	6	31	7	6	292 full	
72	66	6	58	6	27	7	6	298 scant	
66	63	6	62	6	31	7	6	278 full	
66	63	6	61	6	31	7	6	274 scant	
66	63	6	60	6	31	7	6	267 full	
63	60	6	56	6	34	9	6	294......	Trains for nine teeth in scape wheel
66	60	6	54	6	33	9	6	297......	
63	60	6	57	6	34	9	6	299 full	
66	60	6	53	6	33	9	6	291 full	
63	60	6	55	6	34	9	6	289 scant	
60	60	6	52	6	33	9	6	286......	
63	60	6	54	6	34	9	6	283 full	
66	60	6	51	6	33	9	6	280 full	
63	60	6	53	6	34	9	6	278 full	
63	60	6	52	6	34	9	6	273......	
66	60	6	50	6	33	9	6	275......	
58	56	6	53	6	40	11	6	292 full	Trains for eleven teeth in scape wheel.
64	52	6	52	6	30	11	6	294 scant	
60	56	6	52	6	30	11	6	230 scant	
60	60	6	49	6	36	11	6	300 scant	
60	54	6	54	6	40	11	6	397......	
60	54	6	53	6	40	11	6	291 full	
62	54	6	51	6	39	11	6	290 scant	
58	54	6	54	6	41	11	6	287 full	
58	55	6	53	6	41	11	6	287......	
59	54	6	53	6	41	11	6	286 full	
60	54	6	52	6	40	11	6	286......	
61	55	6	51	6	39	11	6	286 scant	

TABLES OF NON-SECOND WATCH TRAINS.

(Continued.)

Centre wheel. No. of teeth in wheel.	3d Wheel and Pinion.		4th Wheel and Pinion.			Scape Wheel and Pinion.		Beats per minute.	Character of trains.
	Teeth in wheel.	Leaves in pin.	Teeth in wheel.	Leaves in Pin.	Seconds in revolutions	Teeth in wheel.	Leaves in pin.	No. of beats.	
56	55	6	50	6	39	11	6	285 scant	
60	55	6	48	6	38	11	6	282 full	
62	54	6	52	6	41	11	6	281 scant	
63	54	6	51	6	40	11	6	281 full	
63	54	6	50	6	39	11	6	280 scant	
70	54	6	54	6	43	11	6	277 full	
70	60	6	48	6	36	11	6	293 full	
70	54	6	52	6	39	11	6	295 full	
60	54	6	50	6	38	11	6	289 scant	
63	48	6	56	6	43	11	6	287 full	Trains for eleven teeth in scape wheel.
63	70	7	56	7	36	11	7	293 full	
80	70	7	48	7	36	11	6	293 full	
80	60	7	48	6	36	11	6	293 full	
80	70	6	48	7	36	11	6	293 full	
80	50	6	56	7	40	11	6	287 full	
80	63	6	50	7	38	11	6	289 scant	
80	80	8	64	8	36	11	8	293 full	
70	80	8	56	8	36	11	7	293 full	
70	80	8	48	8	36	11	6	293 full	
63	56	6	56	7	40	11	6	287 full	
63	64	6	56	8	40	11	6	287 full	
84	48	8	56	6	40	11	6	287 full	
84	56	8	56	7	40	11	6	287 full	
84	64	8	56	8	40	11	6	287 full	
63	63	6	50	7	38	11	6	289 scant	
63	72	6	50	8	38	11	6	289 scant	
84	54	8	50	6	38	11	6	289 scant	
84	63	8	50	7	38	11	6	289 scant	
60	72	8	50	8	38	11	6	289 scant	
70	80	6	48	8	36	11	6	293 full	

TABLES OF NON-SECOND WATCH TRAINS.

(Continued.)

Centre wheel. No. of teeth in wheel.	3d Wheel and Pinion.		4th Wheel and Pinion.			Scape Wheel and Pinion.		Beats per minute.	Character of trains.
No. of teeth in wheel.	Teeth in wheel.	Leaves in pin.	Teeth in wheel.	Leaves in Pin.	Seconds in revolutions	Teeth in wheel.	Leaves in pin.	No. of beats.	
70	80	7	48	8	36	11	6	293 full	Trains for eleven teeth in scape wheel.
80	80	7	56	8	36	11	7	293 full	
80	60	8	48	6	36	11	6	293 full	
80	70	8	48	7	36	11	6	293 full	
80	70	8	56	7	36	11.	7	293 full	
52	52	6	51	6	48	13	6	277 scant	Trains for thirteen teeth in scape wheels.
57	51	6	48	6	44	13	6	280 scant	
56	51	6	49	6	45	13	6	281 scant	
54	52	6	50	6	46	13	6	282 scant	
50	51	6	50	6	45	13	6	284 full	
54	43	6	50	6	45	13	6	287 full	
54	52	6	51	6	46	13	6	287 full	
57	53	6	48	6	43	13	6	291 scant	
56	54	6	48	6	44	13	6	291 full	
56	53	6	49	6	44	13	6	292 scant	
54	53	6	51	6	45	13	6	293 scant	
60	51	6	48	6	42	13	6	294 full	
59	51	6	49	6	43	13	6	296 scant	
56	53	6	50	6	44	13	6	298 scant	
54	53	6	52	6	45	13	6	298 full	
53	52	6	50	6	46	13	6	276 full	
52	52	6	52	6	46	13	6	293 scant	
55	51	6	51	6	46	13	6	287	
56	50	6	51	6	46	13	6	286 full	
56	52	6	48	6	44	13	6	280 full	
56	52	6	50	6	44	13	6	292 full	
60	48	6	48	6	45	13	6	277 full	
60	50	6	48	6	43	13	6	289 scant	
60	54	6	60	8	53	13	6	292 full	
60	58	7	56	7	51	13	6	287 full	

TABLES OF NON-SECOND WATCH TRAINS.

(Continued)

Centre wheel. No. of teeth in wheel.	3d Wheel and Pinion. Teeth in wheel.	3d Wheel and Pinion. Leaves in pin.	4th Wheel and Pinion. Teeth in wheel.	4th Wheel and Pinion. Leaves in Pin.	4th Wheel and Pinion. Seconds in revolutions	Scape Wheel and Pinion. Teeth in wheel.	Scape Wheel and Pinion. Leaves in pin.	Beats per minute. No. of beats.	Character of trains.
60	60	8	54	6	44	13	6	300	Trains for thirteen teeth in scape wheel.
62	56	7	56	7	47	13	6	396 full	
63	52	7	51	6	60	13	6	285	
63	60	7	60	7	60	13	6	290	
64	60	7	60	7	60	13	6	285	
72	70	8	68	8	60	13	6	280	
74	68	8	68	8	60	13	6	286 full	
48	45	6	56	6	50	15	6	288	Trains for fifteen teeth in scape wheel.
48	45	6	57	6	62	15	6	288	
48	45	6	58	6	62	15	6	300	
48	45	6	59	6	60	15	6	291 scant	
58	48	6	46	6	50	15	6	290	
54	50	6	48	6	48	15	6	286	
56	48	6	46	6	50	15	6	289 scant	
63	56	7	56	7	50	15	7	288	
60	56	8	58	7	50	15	6	288	
62	60	8	60	8	50	15	6	288	
72	64	8	50	8	50	15	6	288	
72	64	8	56	8	50	15	7	288	
72	64	8	64	8	50	15	8	288	
52	50	6	48	6	50	15	6	288	
54	48	6	48	6	50	15	6	288	
72	64	8	48	8	50	15	6	288	
72	80	8	64	10	50	15	8	288	
72	80	8	56	10	50	15	7	288	
72	80	8	48	10	50	15	6	288	
63	80	7	64	10	50	15	8	288	
63	80	7	56	10	50	15	7	288	
63	80	7	48	10	50	15	6	288	
..	..	.	..	..	..	.	.	....	

TABLES OF NON-SECOND WATCH TRAINS.

(*Continued.*)

Centre wheel.	3d Wheel and Pinion.		4th Wheel and Pinion.			Scape Wheel and Pinion.		Beats per minute.
No. of teeth in wheel.	Teeth in wheel.	Leaves in pin.	Teeth in wheel.	Leaves in Pin.	Seconds in revolutions	Teeth in wheel.	Leaves in pin.	No. of beats.
72	64	8	56	8	50	17	8	286 scant.
64	64	8	64	8	50	17	8	290 full.
48	48	6	45	6	53	17	6	272 . . . . . .
48	48	6	46	6	53	17	6	278 . . . . . .
64	80	8	48	10	53	17	6	299 full.
54	48	6	44	6	50	17	6	299 full.
51	48	6	45	6	53	17	6	295 full.
54	48	6	43	6	50	17	6	292 full.
48	48	6	48	6	53	17	6	290 full.
51	48	6	45	6	53	17	6	289 . . . . . .
54	48	6	42	6	53	17	6	286 scant.
48	48	6	47	6	53	17	6	284 full.
51	48	6	44	6	53	17	6	283 scant.
64	64	8	60	8	53	17	8	289 scant.
56	56	7	56	7	53	17	7	290 full.
63	56	7	49	7	53	17	7	286 scant.
64	56	8	48	7	53	17	6	290 full.
80	80	10	64	10	53	17	8	290 full.
80	64	10	64	8	53	17	8	290 full.
80	64	10	56	8	53	17	7	290 full.
80	64	10	48	8	53	17	6	290 full.
80	56	10	56	7	.53	17	7	290 full.
80	56	10	48	7	53	17	6	290 full.
64	80	8	64	10	53	17	8	290 full.
64	80	8	56	10	53	17	7	290 full.

Trains for seventeen teeth in scape wheel.

TABLES OF FOURTH WHEEL SECOND WATCH TRAINS.

Centre wheel.	3d Wheel and Pinion.		4th Wheel and Pinion.			Scape Wheel and Pinion.		Beats per minute.	
No. of teeth in wheel.	Teeth in wheel.	Leaves in pin.	Teeth in wheel.	Leaves in Pin.	Seconds in revolutions	Teeth in wheel.	Leaves in pin.	No. of beats.	
48	45	6	76	6	60	11	6	279 scant.	Fourth wheel seconds with eleven teeth in scape wheel.
48	45	6	74	6	60	11	6	271 full.	
48	45	6	71	6	60	11	6	260 full.	
56	60	7	74	8	60	11	6	271 full.	
48	75	6	78	6	60	11	6	286	
60	79	7	74	7	60	11	6	271 full.	
60	79	7	76	7	60	11	6	279 scant.	
60	79	7	78	7	60	11	6	286	
45	56	6	74	7	60	11	6	271 full.	
45	56	6	76	7	60	11	6	279 scant.	
45	56	6	78	7	60	11	6	286	
64	60	8	74	8	60	11	6	271 full.	
64	60	8	76	8	60	11	6	279 scant.	
64	60	8	78	8	60	11	6	286	
60	56	8	74	7	60	11	6	271 full.	
60	56	8	78	7	60	11	6	286	
60	78	8	74	6	60	11	6	271 full.	
48	78	8	78	6	60	11	6	286	
48	60	6	74	8	60	11	6	271 full.	
48	60	6	78	8	60	11	6	286	
60	56	8	76	7	60	11	6	279 scant.	
64	60	8	66	8	60	13	6	286	Fourth wheel seconds with 13 teeth in scape wheel.
64	60	8	67	8	60	13	6	290 full.	
56	75	7	68	10	60	13	6	295 scant.	
45	56	6	66	7	60	13	6	286	
60	49	7	66	7	60	13	6	286	

TABLES OF FOURTH WHEEL SECOND WATCH TRAINS.
(Continued.)

Centre wheel.	3d Wheel and Pinion.		4th Wheel and Pinion.			Scape Wheel and Pinion.		Beats per minute.	
No. of teeth in wheel.	Teeth in wheel.	Leaves in pin.	Teeth in wheel.	Leaves in Pin.	Seconds in revolutions.	Teeth in wheel.	Leaves in pin.	No. of beats.	
60	49	7	77	7	60	13	7	286	Fourth wheel seconds with thirteen teeth in scape wheel.
64	60	8	69	8	60	13	6	299	
64	60	8	68	8	60	13	6	295 scant.	
60	49	7	67	7	60	13	6	290 full.	
48	45	6	66	6	60	13	6	286	
48	45	6	67	6	60	13	6	290 full.	
48	45	6	68	6	60	13	6	284 scant.	
48	45	6	69.	6	60	13	6	299	
60	56	8	66	7	60	13	6	286	
80	60	10	66	8	60	13	6	286	
64	75	8	66	10	60	13	6	286	
48	60	6	66	8	60	13	6	286	
48	75	6	66	10	60	13	6	286	
64	45	8	60	6	60	15	6	300	Fourth wheel seconds with fifteen teeth in scape wheel.
64	60	8	60	8	60	15	6	300	
64	64	8	70	10	60	15	7	300	
64	60	8	70	8	60	15	7	300	
60	56	8	60	7	60	15	6	300	
48	60	6	60	8	60	15	6	300	
60	70	7	70	7	60	15	7	300	
60	49	7	60	7	60	15	6	300	
48	49	6	60	6	60	15	6	300	
80	45	10	70	8	60	15	7	300	
75	60	10	60	8	60	15	6	300	
64	75	7	60	10	60	15	6	300	

TABLES OF FOURTH WHEEL SECOND WATCH TRAINS.

(Continued.)

Centre wheel.	3d Wheel and Pinion.		4th Wheel and Pinion.			Scape Wheel and Pinion.		Beats per minute.	
No. of teeth in wheel.	Teeth in wheel.	Leaves in pin.	Teeth in wheel.	Leaves in Pin.	Seconds in revolutions.	Teeth in wheel.	Leaves in pin.	No. of beats.	
56	75	7	70	10	60	15	7	300	Fourth wheel seconds with fifteen teeth in scape wheel.
56	75	8	60	10	60	15	6	300	
64	75	8	54	8	60	15	6	270	
60	60	8	54	7	60	15	6	270	
64	56	8	54	6	60	15	6	270	
48	45	6	54	8	60	15	6	270	
60	60	7	63	7	60	15	7	270	
60	56	8	48	7	60	15	6	240	
60	49	7	54	7	60	15	6	270	
48	49	6	54	6	60	15	6	270	
64	45	8	48	8	60	15	6	240	
60	60	8	48	7	60	15	6	240	
48	50	6	48	8	60	15	6	240	
64	60	8	48	6	60	15	6	240	
60	45	7	56	7	60	15	7	240	
60	49	7	48	7	60	15	6	240	
48	45	6	48	6	60	15	6	240	
60	56	8	51	7	60	17	6	289	Fourth wheel seconds with seventeen teeth in scape wheel.
64	60	8	50	8	60	17	6	283 full.	
64	60	8	51	8	60	17	6	289	
75	56	10	68	7	60	17	8	289	
80	60	10	50	8	60	17	6	283 full.	
75	64	10	50	8	60	17	6	283 full.	
75	68	10	68	8	60	17	8	289	
80	75	10	68	10	60	17	8	289	

TABLES OF FOURTH WHEEL SECOND WATCH TRAINS.

(Continued.)

No. of teeth in wheel.	Teeth in wheel.	Leaves in pin.	Teeth in wheel.	Leaves in Pin.	Seconds in revolutions.	Teeth in wheel.	Leaves in pin.	No. of beats.	Third wheel and patent second trains.
Centre wheel.	3d Wheel and Pinion.		4th Wheel and Pinion.			Scape Whee and Pinion		Beats per minute.	
60	72	6	60	12	60		6	300	
60	60	6	60	10	60		6	300	
60	48	6	60	8	60		6	300	
48	60	6	60	8	60		6	300	
48	60	6	54	8	60		6	270	
60	72	6	54	12	60		6	270	
48	60	6	48	8	60		6	240	
60	60	6	54	10	60		6	270	
60	72	6	48	12	60		6	240	
48	60	6	48	10	60		6	240	

American Watch.

| 64 | 60 | 8 | 64 | 8 | 60 | 15 | 7 | 300 . . . . . . | |

Trial Watch.

| 80 | 75 | 10 | 80 | 10 | 60 | 15 | 8 | 300 . . . . . . | |

CHAPTER V.

ON TEMPERING.

No part of his trade gives the self-instructed watchmaker more trouble than the acquirement of an ability to temper, as they should be, his various tools and pieces of machinery; in fact a whole life devoted to experiments and study touching this department, would not be likely to attain the desired end. And yet all the processes employed are so amazingly simple as to lead one to wonder, when he understands them, *why* he did not know all about' them before.

TO TEMPER BRASS, OR TO DRAW ITS TEMPER.

Brass is rendered hard by hammering or rolling, therefore when you make a thing of brass, necessary to be in temper, you must prepare the material before shaping the article. Temper may be drawn from brass by heating it to a cherry red, and then simply plunging it into water the same as though you were going to temper steel.

TO TEMPER DRILLS.

Select none but the finest and best steel for your drills. In making them never heat higher than a cherry red, and always hammer till nearly cold. Do all your hammering in one way, for if, after you have flattened your piece out, you attempt to hammer it back to a square or a round you spoil it. When your drill is in proper shape heat it to a cherry red, and thrust it into a piece of resin, or into quicksilver.

Some use a solution of cyanuret potassa and rain-water for tempering their drills, but for my part I have always found the resin or quicksilver to work best.

TO TEMPER GRAVERS.

Gravers and other instruments larger than drills, may be tempered in quicksilver as above; or you may use lead

instead of quicksilver. Cut down into the lead, say half an
inch ; then, having heated your instrument to a light cherry
red, press it firmly into the cut. The lead will melt around
it, and an excellent temper will be imparted.

TO TEMPER CASE SPRINGS.

Having fitted the spring into the case according to your
liking, temper it hard by heating and plunging into water.
Next polish the small end so that you may be able to see
when the color changes ; lay it on a piece of copper or brass
plate, and hold the plate over your lamp, with the blaze
directly under the largest part of the spring. Watch the
polished part of the steel closely, and when you see it turn
blue remove the plate from the lamp, letting all cool gradually together. When cool enough to handle polish the end
of the spring again, place it on the plate and hold over the
lamp as before. The third bluing of the polished end will
leave the spring in proper temper. Any steel article to
which you desire to give a spring temper may be treated in
the same way.

Another process said to be good—I have never tried it—
is to temper the spring as in the first instance; then put it
into a small iron ladle, cover it with linseed oil and hold
over a lamp till the oil takes fire. Remove the ladle, but
let the oil continue to burn until nearly all consumed, when
blow out, re-cover with oil and hold over the lamp as
before. The third burning out of the oil will leave the
spring in the right temper.

TO TEMPER CLICKS, RATCHETS, ETC.

Clicks, ratchets or other steel articles requiring a similar
degree of hardness should be tempered in mercurial ointment. The process consists in simply heating to a cherry
red and plunging into the ointment. No other mode will
combine toughness and hardness to such an extent.

TO DRAW THE TEMPER FROM DELICATE STEEL PIECES
WITHOUT SPRINGING THEM.

Place the articles from which you desire to draw the
temper into a common iron clock key. Fill around it with

brass or iron filings, and then plug up the open end with a steel, iron or brass plug, made to fit closely. Take the handle of the key with your plyers and hold its pipe into the blaze of a lamp till red hot, then let it cool gradually. When sufficiently cold to handle, remove the plug, and you will find the article with its temper fully drawn, but in all other respects just as it was before.

You will understand the reason for having the article thus plugged up while passing it through the heating and cooling process, when I tell you that springing always results from the action of changeable currents of atmosphere. The temper may be drawn from cylinders, staffs, pinions, or any other delicate pieces by this mode with perfect safety.

TO TEMPER STAFFS, CYLINDERS OR PINIONS, WITHOUT SPRINGING THEM.

Prepare the articles as in preceding process, using a steel plug. Having heated the key-pipe to a cherry red, plunge it into water; then polish the end of your steel plug, place the key upon a plate of brass or copper, and hold it over your lamp with the blaze immediately under the pipe till the polished part becomes blue. Let cool gradually, then polish again. Blue and cool a second time, and the work will be done.

TO DRAW THE TEMPER FROM PART OF A SMALL STEEL ARTICLE.

Hold the part from which you wish to draw the temper, with a pair of tweezers, and with your blow-pipe direct the flame upon them—not the article—till sufficient heat is communicated to the article to produce the desired effect.

TO BLUE SCREWS EVENLY.

Take an old watch barrel and drill as many holes into the head of it as you desire to blue screws at a time. Fill it about one-fourth full of brass or iron filings, put in the head, and then fit a wire, long enough to bend over for a handle, into the arbor holes—head of the barrel upwards. Brighten the heads of your screws, set them, point downwards, into the holes already drilled, and expose the bottom of the barrel to your lamp till the screws assume the color you wish

TO REMOVE BLUING FROM STEEL.

Immerse in a pickle composed of equal parts muriatic acid and elixir vitriol. Rinse in pure water and dry in tissue paper.

TO CASE-HARDEN IRON.

Heat to a bright red in a crucible or ladle; pour in enough powdered cyanid of potash to cover it; let remain five or six seconds, and then turn out into rain water. The piece treated in this way will polish up equal to steel, and be almost quite as hard.

—oo꞉ꙩ꞉oo—

CHAPTER VI.

ON MILLS, BROACHES, FILES AND BURNISHERS.

YOUR diamond mills, diamond broaches and diamond files you can generally buy ready made to suit, though instances may occur in which you will require them of a peculiar size and shape, not to be had of the dealers. It is, therefore, best to know how to prepare them. I make all my own for two reasons—they are better than those I can buy, and they do not cost me anything like as much.

To make these articles diamond dust is necessary. This you can buy in most of the large cities ready prepared. It is not a costly article; one dollar's worth will last you a long time.

TO MAKE A DIAMOND MILL.

Make a plain brass wheel about two inches in diameter, and arrange it to work to your foot-lathe. Place it flat on some solid substance, and having oiled its face, sprinkle it thinly with coarse diamond dust. With a smoothe hammer then tap it lightly till the diamond dust is thoroughly driven into the brass. The brass will bur around it and hold it securely in place. We use the oil to prevent the dust from bounding off while undergoing the process of hammering.

A mill prepared in this way will last for years. I have one now in my shop, upon which I have ground watch, spectacle and breastpin glasses for five years, and yet it appears as sharp, and cuts as well as it did at first. As the wheel wears off the diamond grains seem to sink into the brass from the effect of the grinding.

TO MAKE DIAMOND BROACHES.

Make your broaches of brass the size and shape you desire; then, having oiled them slightly, roll their points into fine diamond dust till entirely covered. Hold them then on the face of your anvil and tap with a light hammer till the grains disappear in the brass. Great caution will be necessary in this operation. Do not tap heavy enough to flatten the broach. Very light blows are all that will be required; the grains will be driven in much sooner than one would imagine.

Some roll the broach between two smoothe pieces of steel to imbed the diamond dust. It is a very good way, but somewhat more wasteful of the dust.

Broaches made on this plan are used for dressing out jewels.

TO MAKE POLISHING BROACHES.

These are usually made of ivory, and used with diamond dust, loose, instead of having been driven in. You oil the broach lightly, dip it into the finest diamond dust and proceed to work it into the jewel the same as you do the brass broach. Unfortunately too many watchmakers fail to attach sufficient importance to the polishing broach. The sluggish motion of watches now-a-days, is more often attributable to rough jewels than to any other cause.

TO MAKE DIAMOND FILES.

Shape your file of brass, and charge with diamond dust, as in case of the mill. Grade the dust in accordance with the coarse or fine character of the file desired.

TO MAKE PIVOT FILES.

Dress up a piece of wood file fashion, about an inch

broad, and glue a piece of fine emery paper upon it. Shape
your file then, as you wish it, of the best cast-steel, and
before tempering pass your emery paper heavily across
it several times, diagonally. Temper by heating to a
cherry red, and, plunging into linseed oil. Old worn pivot
files may be dressed over and made new by this process.
At first thought one would be led to regard them too
slightly cut to work well, but not so. They dress a pivot
more rapidly than any other file.

TO MAKE BURNISHERS.

Proceed the same as in making pivot files, with the excep-
tion that you are to use fine flour of emery on a slip of oiled
brass or copper, instead of the emery paper. Burnishers
which have become too smoothe may be improved vastly
with the flour of emery as above without drawing the temper.

TO PREPARE A BURNISHER FOR POLISHING.

Melt a little beeswax on the face of your burnisher. Its
effect then, on brass or other finer metals, will be equal to
the best buff. A small burnisher prepared in this way is
the very thing with which to polish up watch wheels. Rest
them on a piece of pith while polishing.

CHAPTER VII.

ON CLEANING AND REPAIRING CLOCKS.

THE clocks now generally in use among our people are
so simple in their construction, and the processes employed
to keep them in order are so few and plain, that a lengthy
treatise on the subject as indicated by the above heading,
could hardly be profitable. Almost any person endowed
with common sense and a taste for working at light machinery, may, with a little practice, clean and repair clocks
successfully.

With all its simplicity, however, there are many persons
following the business of cleaning and repairing clocks who

do not give satisfaction; or, in other words, who do not seem to possess all the necessary requisites. As an illustration—a man will come to your house, perhaps, take down your clock, clean it properly, repair it all right, put it up as it should be, and then—spoil the job by oiling all the pivots and probably the pinions. The requisite lacking in this case is good common sense. If he had possessed this he would have seen that to oil the pivots or pinions would be to cause their accumulation of dust; that this dust mixing with the oil, must increase the friction by causing the parts to grind together, to say nothing of a gum sure to result —either of which, without the other, could not do otherwise than stop the machine sooner or later,

We often hear persons complaining of their clocks stopping in cold weather—in nine cases out of ten the cause may be attributed to this very injudicious use of oil. A gum has formed on the pivots or pinions, or both, which stiffens under the influence of the cold, and, of course, stops the movement. But this is not the only bad result. A clock grinding along in consequence of having been improperly oiled, will wear out in less than half the time that it would under other circumstances. The reason in this must be apparent to all—each pivot or each pinion leaf has been converted, as it were, into a grindstone.

I am sorry to say that a large per cent. of the professed clock-tinkerers straggling over our country do work on the plan just named. They are generally men who are too lazy to earn an honest living by hard labor, and too dull to do it in any other way. If a man is disposed to work at clocks, and possesses the requirements that will enable him to do it well, a necessity for much "tramping" will never spring up. A community can easily be found that will give him a permanent business. And unless the person applying for a "job" is known, or can furnish satisfactory evidence that he understands his business, and is honest enough to do well what he understands, my advice is to keep him and the clock as far apart as possible. Better ten to one that the owner go to work and put it in repair himself; for certain it is that he will not willfully injure his own property.

Under the impression then that this book may possibly fall into the hands of some who, in consequence of not

being convenient to the establishment of a regular watch
or clock repairer, would like to keep their own clocks in
order, I shall proceed to give a few simple directions, which,
if followed, will enable them to do so without trouble.

TO CLEAN A CLOCK. -

Take the movement of the clock "to pieces." Brush
the wheels and pinions thoroughly with a stiff, coarse brush;
also the plates into which the trains work. Clean the
pivots well by turning in a piece of cotton cloth held tightly
between your thumb and finger. The pivot holes in the
plates are generally cleansed by turning a piece of wood
into them, but I have always found a strip of cloth or a
soft cord drawn tightly through them to act the best. If
you use two cords, the first one slightly oiled, and the next
dry to clean the oil out, all the better. Do not use salt or
acid to clean your clock—it can do no good, but may do a
great deal of harm. Boiling the movement in water, as
some practice, is also foolishness

TO BUSH.

The holes through which the great arbors, or winding
axles work, are the only ones that usually require bushing.
When they have become too much worn the great wheel
on the axle before named strikes too deeply into the pinions
above it, and stops the clock. To remedy this bushing is
necessary, of course. The most common way of doing it is
to drive a steel point or punch into the plate just above the
axle hole, thus forcing the brass downward until the hole is
reduced to its original size. Another mode is to solder a
piece of brass upon the plate in such a position as to hold
the axle down to its proper place. If you simply wish your
clock to run, and have no ambition to produce a bush that
will look workmanlike, about as good a way as any is to fit
a piece of hard wood between the post which comes through
the top of the plate and the axle. Make it long enough to
hold the axle to its proper place, and so that the axle will
run on the end of the grain. Cut notches where the pivots
come through, and secure by wrapping around it and the
plate a piece of small wire, or a thread. There is no post
coming through above the axle on the striking side, but this

will rarely require pushing. I have known clocks to run well on this kind of bushing, botchified as it may appear, for ten years.

TO REMEDY WORN PINIONS.

Turn the leaves or rollers so the worn places upon them will be towards the arbor or shaft, and fasten them in that position. If they are "rolling pinions," and you cannot secure them otherwise, you had better do it with a little soft solder.

TO OIL PROPERLY.

Oil only, and very lightly, the pallets of the verge, the steel pin upon which the verge works, and the point where the loop of the verge wire works over the pendulum wire. Use none but the best watch oil. Though you might be working constantly at the clock-repairing business, a bottle costing you but twenty-five cents, would last you two years at least. You can buy it at any watch-furnishing establishment.

TO MAKE THE CLOCK STRIKE CORRECTLY.

If not very cautious in putting up your clock you will get some of the striking-train wheels in wrong, and thus produce a derangement in the striking. If this should happen, prize the plates apart on the striking side, slip the pivots of the upper wheels out, and having disconnected them from the train, turn them part around and put them back. If still not right, repeat the experiment. A few efforts at most will get them to working properly.

A DEFECT TO LOOK AFTER.

Always examine the pendulum wire at the point where the loop of the verge wire works over it. You will generally find a small notch, or at least a rough place, worn there. Dress it out perfectly smooth, or your clock will not be likely to work well. Small as this defect may seem, it stops a large number of clocks.

CHAPTER VIII.

ON REFINING AND COMPOUNDING METALS.

ALTHOUGH it is not expected that the watchmaker and jeweler will be called upon to do a heavy business in the way of refining metals, yet it is proper for him to know something of the *modus operandi*, for cases may occur in which it will be necessary for him to separate the members of a compound, or to have a metal which he can rely upon as being pure. I shall, therefore, lay before him a few simple recipes. They are not exactly the processes employed when refining is done on a large scale, but they are perfectly reliable, and will answer his purpose ; in fact they are the only ones he could make use of without extensive and expensive preparations.

A thorough knowledge of the formula by which metals are compounded is of the utmost importance.

TO REFINE GOLD.

If you desire to refine your gold from the baser metals, swedge or roll it out very thin, then cut into narrow strips and curl up so as to prevent its lying flatly. Drop the pieces thus prepared into a vessel containing good nitric acid, in the proportion of acid two ounces, and pure rain water half an ounce. Suffer to remain until thoroughly dissolved, which will be the case in from half an hour to one hour. Then pour off the liquid carefully and you will find the gold in the form of a yellow powder lying at the bottom of the vessel. Wash this with pure water till it ceases to have an acid taste, after which you may melt and cast into any form you choose. Gold treated in this way may be relied on as perfectly pure.

In melting gold use none other than a charcoal fire, and during the process sprinkle saltpetre and potash into the crucible occasionally. Do not attempt to melt with stone coal, as it renders the metal brittle and otherwise imperfect.

TO REFINE SILVER.

Dissolve in nitric acid as in the case of the gold. When

the silver has entirely disappeared, add to the two-and-a-half ounces of solution nearly one quart of pure rain water. Sink, then, a sheet of clean copper into it—the silver will collect rapidly upon the copper, and you can scrape it off and melt into bulk at pleasure.

In the event you were refining gold in accordance with the foregoing formula, and the impurity was silver, the only steps necessary to save the latter would be to add the above named proportion of water to the solution poured from the gold, and then to proceed with your copper plate as just directed.

TO REFINE COPPER.

This process differs from the one employed to refine silver in no respects save the plate to be immersed—you use an iron instead of a copper plate to collect the metal.

If the impurities of gold refined were both silver and copper, you might, after saving the silver as above directed, sink your iron plate into the solution yet remaining, and take out the copper. The parts of alloyed gold may be separated by these processes. and leave each in a perfectly pure state.

TO MAKE COIN GOLD.

The gold of American and English coin is twenty-two carat fine. Copper alone usually forms the alloy, though a portion of silver is sometimes added. To make coin gold, you melt together with saltpetre and sal-ammoniac, the two metals in the proportion of twenty-two grains pure gold and two grains pure copper. When silver forms a part of the alloy it is usually about one-third silver to two-thirds copper. The latest American coin is of that alloy.

TO MAKE EIGHTEEN CARAT GOLD

To make the eighteen carat gold, generally in use, melt together as above, eighteen grains pure gold, four grains pure copper and two grains pure silver. In cases where you find it necessary to use gold coin, weigh out in the proportion of nineteen-and-a-half grains gold, three grains copper and one-and-a-half grains silver.

TO MAKE SIXTEEN CARAT GOLD

Compound sixteen grains pure gold with five-and-a-half grains pure copper and two-and-a-half grains pure silver. Or, if gold coin is used, seventeen grains gold, five grains copper and two grains silver.

TO MAKE TWELVE CARAT GOLD.

Melt together, in the usual way, twenty-five grains gold —if coin—thirteen-and-a-half grains copper, and seven-and-a-third grains silver. This is a very good gold for rings, &c.—stands acids almost equal to the higher grades, and looks fully as well. Of course it is deficient in weight.

TO MAKE FOUR CARAT GOLD.

Four carat gold is used to a considerable extent for cheap rings, pin-tongues and the like. It is a very nice metal, wears well, does not black the finger, and presents somewhat the appearance of Guinea gold. You make it by melting together eighteen parts copper, four parts gold, and two parts silver

TO MAKE GREEN GOLD.

Melt together nineteen grains pure gold and five grains pure silver. The metal thus prepared has a beautiful green shade. Some years o it was used pretty extensively by jewelers in the formation of leaves but we do not meet with it so often now.

TO MAKE BEST COUNTERFEIT GOLD.

Fuse together with saltpetre, sal-ammoniac and powdered charcoal, four parts platina, two-and-a-half parts pure copper, one part pure zinc, two parts block tin and one-and-a-half parts pure lead.

Another good recipe calls for two parts platina, one part silver and three parts copper.

A metal compounded in accordance with either formula, as exhibited above, will so nearly resemble gold as to almost defy detection without a resort to thorough tests. The platina requires a high temperature to melt, but nothing could be substituted that would act so well, as it adds to the ring of the metal, and to a great extent fortifies it against the action of acids.

If at any time you should find your metal too hard or brittle for practical use re-melt it with sal-ammoniac. It may in some cases be necessary to repeat this operation several times, but it will be sure to produce the desired effect eventually.

TO MAKE BEST OREIDE-GOLD.

Oreide gold is figuring no little at this time in the way of cheap jewelry. The best article is made by compounding four parts pure copper, one-and-three-fourth parts pure zinc, one-fourth part magnesia, one-tenth part sal-ammoniac, one-twelfth part quick-lime and one part cream tartar. Melt the copper first, then add as rapidly as possible the other articles in the order named.

TO MAKE ALLOYED SILVER.

Copper is the only less precious metal that alloys well with silver. Its addition is a decided improvement on the original, rendering it harder, finer in appearance and more sonorous; and it is astonishing to note the quantity that may be added without otherwise changing the first appearance of the metal. An alloy of silver and copper in the proportion of four-fifths silver to one of copper, is fully as white as the silver would be entirely pure. When the proportion of copper rises above one-fifth, it begins to have an influence in the color. American coin silver is one-tenth copper.

The baser white metals cannot be alloyed with silver to any great extent, owing to the fact that they impart to the compound too great a degree of brittleness. A small proportion of block tin virtually converts it into bell metal.

The following is, perhaps, the best known composition for a cheap silver : Pure silver, say one ounce; copper, one-sixth of an ounce; brass, two-thirds of an ounce; bismuth, one-third of an ounce; clean salt, two-thirds of an ounce; white arsenic, one-third of an ounce; and potash, one-third of an ounce. Melt the silver, copper and brass first, then add the other articles in the order named. Sprinkle a very little borax into the crucible while melting—too much will have a tendency to render the metal unmalleable.

TO MAKE BEST COUNTERFEIT SILVER.

Combine by fusion one part pure copper, twenty-four parts block tin, one-and-a-half parts pure antimony, one-fourth part pure bismuth and two parts clear glass. The glass may be omitted save in cases where it is an object to have the metal sonorous.

TO MAKE GERMAN SILVER.

The best German silver may be made by melting together twenty-five parts copper, fifteen parts zinc and ten parts nickel.

TO MAKE GOLD SOLDER.

Melt together in a charcoal fire twenty-four grains gold coin, nine grains pure silver, six grains copper and three grains good brass. This makes a solder for gold ranging from twelve to sixteen carats in fineness. Where a finer grade is to be worked, the solder may be made to correspond by increasing the proportion of gold in its composition. A darker solder may be made, if desired, by lessening the proportion of silver, and increasing that of the copper in a corresponding degree.

TO MAKE SILVER SOLDER.

The usual method is to combine two parts of silver with one of brass. For my use I generally make the proportion of brass a little larger than one-third. In the course of his work the jeweler invariably throws aside quite a number of cheap pin-tongues as being too soft and too easily bent to be serviceable. Of these I often make my solder, combining them with silver in equal proportion. It seems to work better and more freely than any other I can prepare.

TO MAKE BRASS OR COPPER SOLDER.

Compound in the usual way two parts of brass with one of zinc. Such is the granulated solder sold in the shops under the name of *spelter*.

TO MAKE SOFT SOLDER.

The soft solder used by jewelers is generally a composition of two parts tin and one part lead. A solder composed of two parts bismuth, one part tin and one part lead, flows at a much lower temperature than the above; but it is not so strong.

—◇◇◇—

CHAPTER IX.

ON SOLDERING.

THE first thing to be sure of in making preparations for soldering, is that the compound to be used in uniting the parts is easier of fusion than the parts themselves. Let this be otherwise and the attempt must certainly result in failure. The next thing to look after is the uniformity in the color of the solder and the metal to be soldered; and where such a thing is of importance, the uniformity in point of hardness. To have the color the same is often a matter of no little moment, especially in the case of rings, where the joint would otherwise be made to show. This last, though not least thing in point of consequence, is to see that the surfaces to be joined are perfectly bright and clean. Without this last-named precaution it is impossible to do good work.

TO HARD SOLDER GOLD, SILVER, COPPER, BRASS, IRON, STEEL OR PLATINA.

The solders to be used for gold, silver, copper and brass are given in the preceding chapter. You commence operations by reducing your solder to small particles and mixing it with powdered sal-ammoniac and powdered borax in equal parts, moistened to make it hold together. Having fitted up the joint to be soldered, you secure the article upon a piece of soft charcoal, lay your soldering mixture immediately over the joint, and then with your blow pipe turn the flame of your lamp upon it until fusion takes place. The job is then done and ready to be cooled and dressed up.

Iron is usually soldered with copper or brass in accordance with the above process. The best solder for steel is pure gold or pure silver, though gold or silver solders are often used successfully.

Platina can only be soldered well with gold; and the expense of it, therefore, contributes to the hinderance of a general use of platina vessels, even for chemical purposes, where they are of so much importance.

TO MAKE SOLDERING FLUIDS.

Clip into one ounce of best muriatic acid as much clear sheet zinc as it will dissolve; then add fifteen or twenty grains of sal-ammoniac and half an ounce of pure rain water.

The above fluid is not suitable for iron or steel, on account of the corrosive character of the acid. A soldering fluid may be made for those metals by dissolving chloride of zinc in alcohol. It does not run the solder quite so freely as does the first-named fluid, though it answers a very good purpose. These fluids are only used in soft soldering

TO SOFT SOLDER ARTICLES.

Moisten the parts to be united with soldering fluid; then, having joined them together, lay a small piece of solder upon the joint and hold over your lamp,·or direct the blaze upon it with your blow-pipe until fusion is apparent. Withdraw then from the blaze immediately, as too much heat will render the solder brittle and unsatisfactory. When the parts to be joined can be made to spring or press against each other, it is best to place a thin piece of solder between them before exposing to the lamp.

Where two smooth surfaces are to be soldered one upon the other, you may make an excellent job by moistening them with the fluid, and then, having placed a sheet of tin foil between them, holding them pressed firmly together over your lamp till the foil melts. If the surfaces fit nicely a joint may be made in this way so close as to be almost imperceptibla. The brightest looking lead which comes as a lining to tin boxes works better in the same way than tin foil.

TO CLEANSE GOLD TARNISHED IN SOLDERING.

The old English mode was to expose all parts of the article to a uniform heat, allow it to cool and then boil until bright in urine and sal-ammoniac. It is now usually cleansed with diluted sulphuric acid. The pickle is made in about the proportion of one-eighth of an ounce acid to one ounce rain water.

TO CLEANSE SILVER TARNISHED IN SOLDERING.

Some expose to a uniform heat, as in the case of gold, and then boil in strong alum water. Others immerse for a considerable length of time in a liquid made of half an ounce of cyanuret potassa to one pint rain water, and then brush off with prepared chalk.

CHAPTER X.

ON PLATING.

To plate, according to the original meaning, was to solder a thin layer of gold or silver upon a baser metal, and then roll out the two together. In later days a broader meaning has been given to the word, so that any method of laying a finer metal upon a coarser is known as plating. There are now various modes of doing this, all of which are more or less interesting and useful to the watchmaker and jeweler.

TO MAKE GOLD SOLUTION FOR ELECTRO-PLATING.

Dissolve five pennyweights gold coin, five grains pure copper and four grains pure silver in three ounces nitro-muriatic acid; which is simply two parts muriatic acid and one part nitric acid. The silver will not be taken into solution as are the other two metals, but will gather at the bottom of the vessel. Add one ounce pulverized sulphate of iron, half an ounce pulverized borax, twenty-five grains pure table salt, and one quart hot rain water. Upon this the gold and copper will be thrown to the bottom of the vessel with the silver. Let stand till fully settled, then pour off the liquid carefully, and refill with boiling rain water as before. Continue to repeat this operation until the precipitate is thoroughly washed; or, in other words, fill up, let settle, and pour off so long as the accumulation at the bottom of the vessel is acid to the taste.

You now have about an eighteen carat chloride of gold. Add to it an ounce and an eighth cyanuret potassa, and one quart rain water—the latter heated to the boiling point. Shake up well, then let stand about twenty-four hours and it will be ready for use.

Some use platina as an alloy instead of silver, under the impression that plating done with it is harder. I have used both, but never could see much difference.

Solution for a darker colored plate to imitate Guinea gold may be made by adding to the above one ounce of dragon's blood and five grains iodide of iron.

If you desire an alloyed plate, proceed as first directed, without the silver or copper, and with an ounce and a half of sulphuret potassa in place of the iron, borax and salt.

TO MAKE SILVER SOLUTION FOR ELECTRO-PLATING.

Put together into a glass vessel, one ounce good silver, made thin and cut into strips; two ounces best nitric acid and half an ounce pure rain water. If solution does not begin at once, add a little more water—continue to add a very little at a time till it does. In the event it starts off well, but stops before the silver is fully dissolved, you may generally start it up again all right by adding a little more water.

When solution is entirely effected, add one quart of warm rain water and a large tablespoonful of table salt. Shake well and let settle, then proceed to pour off and wash through other waters as in the case of the gold preparation. When no longer acid to the taste, put in an ounce and an eighth cyanuret potassa and a quart pure rain water; after standing about twenty-four hours it will be ready for use.

TO PLATE WITH A BATTERY.

If the plate is to be gold use the gold solution for electro-plating; if silver, use the silver solution. Prepare the article to be plated by immersing it for several minutes in a strong ley made of potash and rain water, polishing off thoroughly at the end of the time with a soft brush and prepared chalk. Care should be taken not to let the fingers come in contact with the article while polishing, as that has a tendency to prevent the plate from adhering—it should be held in two or three thicknesses of tissue paper.

Attach the article, when thoroughly cleansed, to the positive pole of your battery, then affix a piece of gold or silver, as the case may be, to the negative pole, and immerse both into the solution in such a way as not to hang in contact with each other.

After the article has been exposed to the action of the battery about ten minutes, take it out and wash or polish over with a thick mixture of water and prepared chalk or jeweler's rouge. If, in the operation, you find places where the plating seems inclined to peel of, or when it has not taken well, mix a little of the plating solution with prepared chalk or rouge, and rub the defective part thoroughly with it. This will be likely to set all right.

Govern your time of exposing the article to the battery by the desired thickness of the plate. During the time it should be taken out and polished up as just directed about every ten minutes, or as often at least as there is an indication of a growing darkness on any part of its surface. When done, finish with the burnisher on prepared chalk and chamois skin, as best suits your taste and convenience.

In case the article to be plated is iron, steel, lead, pewter, or block tin, you must, after first cleansing with the ley and chalk, prepare it by applying with a soft brush—a camel's hair pencil is best suited—a solution made of the following articles in the proportion named :—Nitric acid, half an ounce ; muriatic acid, one third of an ounce ; sulphuric acid, one ninth of an ounce ; muriatic of potash, one seventh of an ounce ; sulphate of iron, one fourth of an ounce ; sulphuric ether, one fifth of an ounce, and as much sheet zinc as it will dissolve. This prepares a foundation, without which the plate would fail to take well, if at all.

TO PLATE WITHOUT A BATTERY.

Prepare the article same as to plate with a battery, then attach to a strip of sheet zinc and suspend in the gold or silver solution for electro-plating as the case may be. The zinc is usually passed around the object to be plated, though this is of no particular importance, all that is necessary is to have the metals in actual contact. Observe the same rules as laid down in the directions for plating with a battery. If the article being plated has the strip of zinc touching much of its surface, it may be well to change the place of contact at every polishing.

You will find this mode of plating but little inferior to that of plating with a battery. It is more employed now, perhaps, than any other.

TO MAKE GOLD AMALGAM.

Eight parts of gold and one of mercury are formed into an amalgam for plating by rendering the gold into thin plates, making it red hot and then putting it into the mercury while the latter is also heated to ebullition. The gold immediately disappears in combination with the mercury, after which the mixture may be turned into water to cool. It is then ready for use.

TO PLATE WITH GOLD AMALGAM.

Gold amalgam is chiefly used as a plating for silver, copper or brass. The article to be plated is washed over with diluted nitric acid or potash ley and prepared chalk, to remove any tarnish or rust that might prevent the amalgam from adhering. After having been polished perfectly bright the amalgam is applied as evenly as possible, usually with a fine scratch brush. It is then set upon a grate over a charcoal fire, or placed into an oven and heated to that degree at which mercury exhales. The gold, when the mercury has evaporated, presents a dull yellow color. Cover it with a coating of pulverized nitre and alum in equal parts, mixed to a paste with water, and heat again till *it* is thoroughly melted, then plunge into water. Burnish up with a steel or bloodstone burnisher.

TO MAKE AND APPLY GOLD PLATING SOLUTION.

Dissolve half an ounce of gold amalgam in one ounce of nitro-muriatic acid. Add two ounces of alcohol, and then, having brightened the article in the usual way, apply the solution with a soft brush. Rinse and dry in saw-dust, or with tissue paper, and polish up with chamois skin.

TO MAKE AND APPLY GOLD PLATING POWDERS.

Prepare a chloride of gold the same as for plating with a

battery. Add to it when thoroughly washed out, cyanuret potassa in the proportion of two ounces to five pennyweights of gold. Pour in a pint of clean rain water, shake up well and then let stand till the chloride is dissolved. Add then one pound of prepared Spanish whiting and let evaporate in the open air till dry, after which put away in a tight vessel for use. To apply it you prepare the article in the usual way, and having made the powder into a paste with water, rub it upon the surface with a piece of chamois skin or cotton flannel.

An old mode of making a gold plating powder was to dip clean linen rags into solution prepared as in the second article preceding this, and having dried, to fire and burn them into ashes. The ashes formed the powder, and were to be applied as above.

TO MAKE AND APPLY SILVER PLATING SOLUTION.

Put together in a glass vessel one ounce nitrate of silver, two ounces cyanuret potassa, four ounces prepared Spanish whiting and ten ounces pure rain water. Cleanse the article to be plated as per preceding directions, and apply with a soft brush. Finish with the chamois skin or burnisher.

TO MAKE AND APPLY SILVER PLATING POWDER.

Dissolve silver in nitric acid by the aid of heat; put some pieces of copper into the solution to precipitate the silver; wash the acid out in the usual way; then with fifteen grains of it mix two drachms of tartar, two drachms of table salt and half a drachm of pulverized alum. Brighten the article to be plated with ley and prepared chalk, and rub on the mixture. When it has assumed a white appearance exposo to heat as in the case of plating with gold amalgam, then polish up with the burnisher or soft leather.

TO SILVER IVORY.

Immerse the ivory in a weak solution of nitrate of silver till it takes upon itself a bright yellow color; take it then from the solution and expose, under water, to the rays of the sun. In two or three hours it will become black; but on taking it out of the water and rubbing it, the blackness will change to a beautiful silvering.

TO SILVER GLASS GLOBES.

Take equal parts of tin and lead, and melt them together; add while they are in fusion two parts of bismuth and two parts of mercury. Take from the fire, and so soon as cool enough for the glass to bear it, pour into the globe and move slowly so that the amalgam will pass over every part of its interior. A thin film will be left at every point of contact.

CHAPTER XI.

MISCELLANEOUS RECIPES.

TO FROST WATCH MOVEMENTS.

Sink that part of the article to be frosted for a short time in a compound of nitric acid, muriatic acid and table salt— one ounce of each. On removing from the acid, place it in a shallow vessel containing enough sour beer to merely cover it, then with a fine scratch brush scour thoroughly, letting it remain under the beer during the operation. Next wash off, first in pure water and then in alcohol. Gild or silver in accordance with any recipe in the chapter on plating.

TO MAKE CLEANSING SOLUTION FOR BRASS.

Put together two ounces sulphuric acid, an ounce and a half nitric acid, one dram saltpetre and two ounces rain water. Let stand for a few hours, and apply by passing the article in and out quickly, and then washing off thoroughly with clean rain water. Old discolored brass chains treated in this way will look equally as well as when new. The usual method of drying is in sawdust.

TO MAKE AND APPLY SOLUTION FOR FROSTING SILVER ARTICLES.

Put one dram of sulphuric acid into four ounces of rain water. Heat the solution and sink the silver in it till frosted as desired then wash clean and dry in sawdust. Half a dram of acid to four ounces water makes a good solution for whitening silver articles.

POLISHING POWDER FOR GOLD ARTICLES.

Dr. W. Hofman has analyzed a polishing powder sold by gold workers in Germany, which always commands a very high price, and hence, it may be inferred, is well adapted for the purpose. He found it to be a very simple composition, being a mixture of about 70 per cent. of sesquioxide of iron and 30 per cent. of sal-ammoniac. To prepare it, protochloride of iron, prepared by dissolving iron in hydrochloric acid, is treated with liquid ammonia until a precipitate is no longer formed. The precipitate is collected on a filter, and without washing, is dried at such a temperature that the adhering sal-ammoniac shall not be volatilized. The peroxide of iron precipitate at first becomes charged with sesquioxide.

TO REMOVE TARNISH FROM ELECTRO-PLATED GOODS.

Make a solution of half a pound cyanuret potassa in two gallons rain water. Immerse the article till the tarnish has disappeared, then rinse off carefully in three or four waters, and dry in sawdust.

TO MAKE RED WATCH HANDS.

Mix together and hold over a lamp, until formed into a paste, one ounce carmine, one ounce muriate of silver and half an ounce tinner's japan. Apply to the watch hands, lay them on a copper plate, face up, and then hold the plate over your spirit lamp till they assume the color you desire.

TO GIVE PLASTER FIGURES THE APPEARANCE OF BRONZE.

Make a preparation of palm soap, five ounces; sulphate of copper, one and a half ounces, and sulphate of iron, one and a half ounces. Dissolve the soap in rain water in one vessel and the sulphates in another. Put together and let settle, then pour off the water. Dry the precipitate, and apply to the figure by mixing as a paint with linseed oil and turpentine.

TO ETCH ON IVORY,

Cover the ivory to be etched with a thin coating of beeswax, then trace the figure you desire to present through the
wax. Pour over it a strong solution of nitrate of silver.
Let remain a sufficient length of time, then remove it, with
the wax, by washing in warm water. The design will be
left in dark lines on the ivory.

TO ENAMEL GOLD OR SILVER.

Take half a pennyweight of silver, two pennyweights and
a half of copper, three pennyweights and a half of lead
and two pennyweights and a half of muriate of ammonia.
Melt together and pour into a crucible with twice as much
pulverized sulphur; the crucible is then to be immediately
covered that the sulphur may not take fire, and the mixture
is to be calcined over a smelting fire until the superfluous
sulphur is burned away. The compound is then to be
coarsely pounded, and with a solution of muriate of ammonia
to be formed into a paste, which is to be placed upon the
article it is designed to enamel. The article must then be
held over a spirit lamp till the compound upon it melts and
flows. After this it may be smoothed and polished up in
safety. This makes the black enamel now so much used on
jewelry.

TO DESTROY THE EFFECT OF ACIDS ON CLOTHES.

Dampen as soon as possible after exposure to the acid
with spirits ammonia. It will destroy the effect immediately.

TO WASH SILVER WARE.

Never use a particle of soap on your silver ware, as it
dulls the lustre, giving the article more the appearance of
pewter than silver. When it wants cleaning rub it with
a piece of soft leather and prepared chalk, the latter made
into a kind of paste with pure water. I say pure water, for
the reason that water not pure might contain gritty particles.

TO CLEANSE BRUSHES.

The best method of cleansing watchmakers' and jewelers'
brushes is to wash them out in strong soda water. When

the oacks are wood you must favor that part as much as possible, for being glued the water may injure them.

TO CUT GLASS ROUND OR OVAL WITHOUT A DIAMOND.

Scratch the glass around the shape you desire with the corner of a file or graver; then, having bent a piece of wire to the same shape, heat it red hot and lay it upon the scratch, sink the glass into cold water just deep enough for the water to come almost on a level with its upper surface. It will rarely ever fail to break perfectly true.

TO RE-BLACK CLOCK HANDS.

Use asphaltum varnish. One coat will make old rusty hands look as good as new, and it dries in a very few minutes.

GLOSSARY.

ARBOR.—An axle which turns upon itself by means of its pivots. Some watchmakers apply the term only to the post on which the key is placed to wind the watch, and to the rod passing through the cannon.

ANCHOR.—A piece of the escapement used in clocks and lever watches.

ANCHOR ESCAPEMENT WATCH.—A detached lever is often called an anchor escapement.

BARREL.—That piece of the watch which contains the main spring.

BRIDGE.—A piece secured to the plate, in which a pivot works, as in the case of skeleton levers.

BALANCE.—A wheel which moves back and forth in obedience to the adverse action of the lever and hair spring.

BEAT.—Each "tick" of the watch is called a beat.

CLICK.—A small lever which works into a ratchet and prevents the sudden recoil of the mainspring when the watch is wound up.

CENTRE WHEEL.—The large wheel immediately in the centre of the watch.

CHICK.—A small pin; usually those which hold the bridges in position.

CYLINDER.—The hollow piece which checks the onward motion of the scape wheel in cylinder escapement watches.

CANNON.—The steel piece which comes up through the dial, and around which the hour wheel revolves. In English and American levers the minute hand is fastened upon it.

COMMON PINION.—The pinion at the lower end of the cannon, which moves the minute wheel.

COCK.—Bridge over the balance.

COLLET.—A small ring fitting on the balance staff or arbor, and holding the inside end of the hair spring. The rings into which jewels are sometimes set are also called collets.

DIAL.—The face of the watch or clock.

DIAL WHEELS.—Those working between the dial and pillar plate.

DEPTHING TOOL.—An instrument used for finding the proper location of pivot holes.

ESCAPEMENT.—Those pieces in the watch or clock which work together and regulate the velocity of the time train.

ELECTRO PLATING—Plating through the aid of electricity. Formerly it was only done with a battery, but recent discoveries enable us to make a very good electro-plate without a battery.

FUSEE.—The cone-shaped wheel upon which the chain works.

FOURTH WHEEL.—The wheel which, in ordinary watches, works into the scape wheel.

FOURTH WHEEL SECOND.—A watch carrying a second hand on the pivot of its fourth wheel.

FORK.—That part of the lever into which the ruby pin plays.

FLY.—An arbor carrying two wings for the purpose of meeting with atmospheric resistance, and thus regulating the motion of striking trains in clocks.

GUARD POINT.—The wedge-shaped elevation immediately back of the fork in detached levers.

GEARING.—The action of the teeth of one wheel upon those of another wheel or pinion.

HOROLOGY.—That branch of science which treats of the principles and construction of machines for measuring time.

HOROLOGIST.—One who interests himself in the science of horology. A constructor or repairer of machines for measuring time. Strictly applicable to the American watch maker, owing to the fact that he works on all manner of time machines.

HOUR WHEEL.—The wheel working around the cannon, and upon which the hour hand is fastened.

INDEX.—Hand.

JEWEL.—The stone or glass settings through which or against which the pivots work; also the settings in the pallets and the roller.

LEAVES.—Teeth or cogs of a pinion.

LEVER.—A horizontal bar upon which the pallets are secured, and which conducts the effect of the motive power from the train to the balance.

MINUTE WHEEL.—A name generally given to that dial wheel which is driven by the cannon pinion.

MOVEMENT.—The interior works of the clock or watch, independent of case.

PALLETS.—The jeweled piece of the lever watch which works into the teeth of the scape wheel.

PIVOT.—The end of an arbor turned very small to avoid friction.

PINION.—A small leaved wheel.

PILLARS.—Posts which in plate watches hold the plates the proper distance apart for the working of the train or trains between them.

PILLAR PLATE.—Usually the bottom plate of a watch, but European watchmakers generally call both pillar plates, distinguishing them as the upper and lower.

PUTTING UP.—Setting the different parts of a clock or watch into their proper places.

PIVOT WOOD.—A tough wood employed by watchmakers in cleaning out pivot holes. It is sometimes called peg wood. A scape wheel is sometimes called a ratchet in Europe.

RATCHET.—A steel wheel into which the click works.

RUBY PIN.—A small glass or stone pin which works in connection with the lever.

ROLLER.—The circular plate into which the ruby pin is set. It is often called the ruby pin table.

ROLL PLATE.—The best grade of plated jewelry.

STOP WORKS.—A mechanism to prevent the watch from being wound up too far.

STAFF.—A name generally applied to the balance arbor of lever watches; also to the arbor passing through the pallets.

SCAPE WHEEL.—The last wheel of the train.

SECOND WATCHES.—Watch with a second hand.

SCRATCH BRUSH.—A brush made of fine brass wire.

TEETH —Cogs by which the motion of one wheel is communicated to another.

TRAIN.—A collection of wheels so arranged that the moving power applied to the first wheel is freely communicated to them all.

THIRD WHEEL.—The wheel into whose pinion the centre wheel works.

TAKING DOWN.—Taking apart the different pieces of a clock or watch.

WHEEL BED.—A bed turned out in the plate of a watch to receive a wheel.

SUPPLEMENT

AMERICAN WATCHMAKER AND JEWELER;

CONTAINING

ADDITIONAL VALUABLE INFORMATION,

INCLUDING

PRIVATE FORMULAS AND PROCESSES OF LEADING AMERICAN HOUSES,

TOGETHER WITH

A CAREFUL SELECTION OF THE BEST FRENCH AND ENGLISH METHODS, ADAPTED TO THE AMERICAN TRADE.

————∘∘⦂⊗⦂∘∘————

PUBLISHERS' NOTE.

SINCE its first publication, some five years ago, the foregoing work has passed through several editions and has received the very strong approval of practical watchmakers and jewelers. During this time we have sought among those best versed in the secrets of the trade, as well as in foreign publications, for any additional information which would add to the value of our book. Our labors have been rewarded by the matter which we present in the following supplemental pages.

Therein will be found the private processes of leading houses in this city, as well as secrets which have been sold at high prices by their inventors, discoverers, or lucky finders. For some of these we were obliged to pay amounts which would seem extravagant did we not know their great value to the trade. From foreign sources we have also added a carefully revised selection of favorite standard recipes, adapted to the use of American workmen.

With these additions we are confident our book will be found a complete and reliable guide, and to repay many times it cost, not only as an instructor in things which may not already be known, but as a convenient reminder from time to time.

SUPPLEMENT.

PRIVATE FORMULAS AND PROCESSES

OF

LEADING AMERICAN JEWELERS.

TO MELT FROM ONE TO THIRTY DWTS. OF ANY K. GOLD WITHOUT THE USE OF A FORGE.

PREPARE a piece of charcoal about a foot long and two or three inches wide ; anneal it in order to remove the air from it, and prevent it snapping ; flatten one side by grinding on some flat surface. Dig a hole deep enough near one end, to hold the quantity you wish to melt. Now cut a strip of sheet iron, about an eighth of an inch wide and long enough to bend an ingot. Say you want to cast a bar. one inch wide. Bend the strip this shape ⊏. Take a piece of sheet iron and cover the ingot ; place both of them on the charcoal, the opening near the hole in the coal. Bind tightly with iron binding wire all together. Put the gold in the hole of coal, and fuse with the blow-pipe. Then incline the coal, which you hold in your left hand, the gold will pass in the ingot. This gold will be tough. By bending a number of ingots and keeping them on hand, you will save much time. They can be used a number of times.

TO MELT GOLD ALLOYS FOR JEWELERS' USE.

Make a good fire, either in forge or furnace. Heat the ingot in which you wish to cast the gold a little hotter than boiling water ; now put the alloy in the Hessian crucible, and after adding a small amount of pulverized borax, put in and leave in the fire until melted. Cast this in any ingot which is clean, and after breaking the bar in pieces small enough to put in the pot again, remelt the gold, do not add any borax this time, but when the gold looks clear and smooth on the top, add (for six ozs. gold) a piece of saltpetre about the size of a pea, and in about half a minute pour the gold. Be sure and keep up the heat after adding the saltpetre—then pour a few drops of oil into the iron ingot; shake it out, and pour the gold. If the gold, silver and copper were clean when you commenced, the gold will roll well. Much depends on the first rolling of the stock; 18 k. should be subjected to a very heavy strain, the first and second draughts. This gives a grain to the stock; light draughts stretch the gold on the surface and the middle portion remaining as cast, causes the gold to crack, many good bars have been condemned when the difficulty was in the rolling. After the 18 k. has been rolled to about twice its length, it must be annealed, then rolled to the size you need.

When you melt 14 k., proceed as with 18 k. Give it as heavy strains in the mills, but do not roll as much before annealing as the 18 k.

The other carats, of lower grade do not require the use of saltpetre to toughen, instead of which, use a small amount of sal ammoniac, proceed then as in the other carats.

When you anneal red gold, do not quench when red hot, as it will cause it to slit or seam; allow the gold to blacken before quenching.

Always melt new alloys twice, and do the same with solders, as the copper may not be thoroughly mixed the first melting; and if it is not, it will show in streaks in the gold, and the solder will not flow.

TO PREPARE GOLD SOLUTION FOR ELECTRO-PLATING WITHOUT THE USE OF ACIDS.

Dissolve 4 ozs. cyanide of potassium in a gallon of soft water. Heat this solution, and after having placed a small porous cell in it, and filled the cell with the solution, put in the cell a plate of copper, to which is attached the wire from the zinc plate of battery; then fasten the wire running from the platina of battery, to a gold plate the size of the copper plate in the porous cell. Keep the solution hot and see that the battery is in good working order. The current will pass through the porous cup, but the gold will not adhere to it, but will be taken in the solution. Weigh your gold occasionally, and when the difference in weight shows 8 or 10 dwts., the solution is charged enough. Now add as much water as has evaporated, and add a little more cyanide; filter through paper, by the aid of a glass funnel, and your solution is ready; this is the best way to make it, and if properly used will last for years.

The zinc plates of battery should be amalgamated with quicksilver. It preserves the zinc and makes the flow of galvanism more regular. This can be done by dipping the zinc in a weak pickle of vitriol and water, and then pouring a few drops of quicksilver on it. Rub with a piece of cotton batting until they are covered, then shake all the quicksilver off. Put the battery together, and see that there is no action unless the poles are connected. It is now ready to use.

TO REMOVE THE DEVIL OR TIN FROM THE STOCK.

Just before pouring the gold throw a small piece of corrosive sublimate in the pot, stir well with a long piece of pointed charcoal, and allow the pot to remain on the fire about half a minute afterward. This will take tin from the alloy; while the tin is in, the gold *will not roll* without cracking.

To remove emery or steel filings, &c., from gold, when melting, use a small piece of glass-gall, it will collect them in the flux.

TOUCH STONE.

Obtain a piece of silica or "black stone," as it is called, from the lapidary and have it made smooth on one side. Solder on the ends of brass wire a small piece of 4, 5, 6, 7, 8, 9, 10, 11, 12, 13, 14, 15, 16, 17, 18, 20, 22, k. gold. You may not need all of these, 10, 12, 14, 16, 18, 20, 22, k. will answer. Be sure that these pieces are alloyed correctly. Take the gold you wish to test, rub it on the stone, the same as you would rub a pencil on paper, it will leave a streak. Now after forming something of an estimate by its looks, as to its quality, (suppose you think it 14 k.) rub point 16 k. on one side and 12 k. on the other,

and place the acid on each streak the same instant. If the
12 k. streak disappears first, the object streak next, and 16
k. last, you may infer that the gold is better than 12 k. and
poorer than 16 k. Try again with 13 k. and 15 k. and
judge as before.

TESTING.

The acid to be used is nitric, slightly diluted, with the
addition of a small quantity of salt. You should have two
or three bottles containing fluid of different strength; for
22 to 18, use the above; for lesser grades dilute with more
water. After a little practice a good observer can arrive
within half a carat of the quality.

CHARCOAL ASSAY.

By this process an assay accurate enough for small
quantities, can be made in a short time. Suppose you have
melted and refined some gold filings, you now have the
gold and silver, and wish to know the carat. Try it on the
"touch-stone" and approximate its quality. Weigh *very*
carefully 12 grains; reduce this by means of fine silver to
8 k, or a little less; melt this into a shot and flatten on a
clean piece of steel, then anneal and roll into a thin ribbon,
coil it loosely like a watch spring, then anneal and put in a
glass retort; cover with nitric acid one-half, water one-
half; boil for 10 minutes, then pour off the solution, and
use three-fourths acid and one-fourth water, boil as before
10 minutes, pour off the solution again, rinse well and then
boil for five minutes in pure nitric acid; rinse several
times with hot water. Dry the gold and melt it into a shot,
then weigh this shot. Twice the weight will be the carat of
the metal. It is unnecessary to say that the utmost care
must be taken as to weight and the manipulations to succeed in arriving at accurate results by this process.

TO REMOVE QUICKSILVER FROM RINGS, CHAINS, &c.

Sometimes quicksilver will get on a piece of work and
completely cover it, This makes the article very brittle,
as well as spoiling its appearance. Heat the article
gradually and under the spot where quicksilver is on—
avoid the fumes. It will entirely remove it.

TO TAKE ENAMEL OUT OF WORK WITHOUT ANNEAL-ING IT.

Take fluor-spar, and pound it fine, use enough of the powder to cover well the article, then take a *lead cup* and pour vitriol on sufficient to make a thin liquid. Boil the article in this, the enamel will be removed. Be very careful and let the fumes pass up chimney, as they are injurious.

TO MAKE PLATED STOCK.

Cast the bar of gold which you wish to plate, the width you desire and roll to the thickness of an eighth of an inch. Should you want to plate on silver, cast the silver the same width as the gold and roll a little longer than the gold. Usually the lower grade metal is two or three times the thickness of the better, therefore use as much as will make the proportion desired. Planish as nearly flat and straight as possible, then file one face of silver and one face of gold until they are bright.

Previous to this you have rolled a piece of plate solder very thin, say 36 in round size plate, and cut a strip a little wider and a little longer than your gold. Emery paper can be used to clean each side of this from dirt, &c. Cover the surface with ground borax from the slate, on each side; do the same on the bright faces of the gold and silver, place the solder. between them, the same as meat in a sandwich Have a piece of iron wire about three-eighths of an inch in thickness and three feet long, ready, place this lengthwise on the gold and squeeze the whole tightly together in a vice. Now bind, with heavy binding wire every inch or so, the whole together. Make a good charcoal fire in the forge, build it so as to be like an oven and then solder; when the solder melts on each side the whole length, the thing is done. then roll as other stock. If you are making gold plating, that is 18 k. or 16 k. on 14 k. and 12 k., you must use a gold solder about 5 or 6 kts.. less than the inferior gold. If gold on silver or composition, use copper solder as per alloys.

The clippings from above when the gold is on silver, may be placed in an enameled vessel and covered with nitric acid, 2 parts; water, 1 part. The silver will be taken in solution which must be saved in an earthen pot. The silver can be collected by precipitating with salt, or after the solution has been diluted, a bar of copper placed in it will collect it, this must be well washed and dried, then melted. The gold after being well dried can be melted in a bar, a small amount of copper may be added. It will then be of the same quality as before.

TO CLOSE CRACKS IN CORAL, &c.

Warm coral very carefully, and with a pencil brush cover the crack with watch oil; when cool the seam will not show.

RULE FOR ALLOYING BY WHICH ANY K. CAN BE MADE FROM FINE GOLD.

Fine or pure gold is 24 carats.

Multiply the number of dwts. you wish to use of fine gold, by 24, the product will be the number of dwts. of 1 k. which it will make. Divide this product by the k. you want to make, then subtract the weight of gold from the dividend, the remainder will be the amount of alloy to be used. Should you want the gold to be yellow—make one-half of the alloy silver, the other half copper. If pale, a little less copper than silver. If red, so as to obtain a good color by the wet color process, make most of the alloy copper, as it is dissolved easier than the silver, by the color.

Example.—Suppose you have 70 dwts. of fine gold and wish to make 14 k. to use for Etruscan work.

$$\begin{array}{l} \text{70 dwts. the weight.} \\ \underline{\text{24 k. the quality.}} \\ \text{1680 number of dwts. of 1 k.} \end{array}$$

$$14)1680(120 \text{ number of dwts, of 1 k.}$$
$$\underline{\qquad}\quad 70 \text{ number of dwts of 24 k.}$$
$$\overline{\quad\;\; 50} \text{ alloy to be added.}$$

The alloy for 14 k. red, to be colored should be as 4 copper to 1 silver; therefore we will take 40 dwts. copper, and 10 dwts. silver. [See 14 k. alloy.]

Should you wish to make polished work of 14 k. the copper should be as 3 to 2. If pale ½ copper and ½ silver. [See alloys.]

Should you use American gold, multiply the weight by 21¾ k., or if you use sovereigns, multiply the weight by 22 k.

These alloys may be made in ozs., dwts., or grs.

18 k., French alloy and first rate color : 150 gold, 23 silver, 27 copper.

18 k.—Red gold to color : 90 gold, 5 silver, 25 copper.

16 k.—64 gold, 15 silver, 17 copper.

16 k.—Red gold to color : 64 gold, 7 silver, 25 copper.

14 k.—140 gold, 40 silver, 60 copper.

14 k.—Red gold to color : 70 dwts., 10 silver, 40 copper.

12 k.—120 gold, 50 silver, 70 copper

12 k —Red gold to color : 120 gold, 30 silver, 90 copper.

10 k.—100 gold, 60 silver, 80 copper.

10 k.—Red gold : 100 gold, 50 silver, 90 copper.

SOLDERS FOR THE ABOVE.

For 18 k.—14 grs., gold, 6 grs., silver, 4 grs., copper.

For 18 k.—Red gold to color ; 14 grs., gold, 5 grs., silver, 5 copper.

Another.—Take 24 grs., of the 18 k., alloyed gold, 6 grs. silver.

For 16 k.—12 grs. gold, 7 silver, 5 copper.

For 16 k.—Red gold to color : 12 grs. gold, 7 silver, 5 copper.

Another.—Take of the 16 k. alloyed gold, 24 grs , 6 grs. silver

For 14 k.—10 grs., gold, 8 grs., silver, 6 grs , copper.

For 14k.—Red gold to color: 10 grs gold, 8 silver, 6 coppper.

Another.—Take 24 grs. of 14k alloyed gold 6 grs. silver.

Always melt solders twice ; break the first bar in pieces, and put in the pot while pot is hot.

Solders used on any quality of gold better than their own carat :—

7½k Solder, usually called 8 k.—7½ dwts. gold, 9¾ silver, 1¼ copper. To make this flow very easy add 15 grs. brass, (second melting).

5 k. Solder.—5 dwts., gold, 13 silver, 6 copper; add 15 grs. brass second melting.

3½ k. Solder usually called 2 k.—1 dwt. gold, 1 copper, 1 brass, 4 silver coin ; add brass on second melting.

The above solder will flow easier than copper solder and is very useful for repairing, &c , &c.

Copper solder.—16 dwts coin silver, 3 copper, 1 brass. Should this solder be required to flow very easy, add a little arsenic on second melting.

COLORING.

Wet color for Etruscan-gold jewelry, French color.— 8 ozs. saltpetre, 8 ozs. salt, 6 muriatic acid, 2 soft water.

American color is almost alike :—8 ozs. saltpetre, 4 ozs. salt, 2 ozs. sal am. 4 ozs. muriatic acid, 2 ozs. water. Same treatment as below.

This is sufficient for 6 ozs. jewelry. The work which has been annealed, boiled in sulphuric or muriatic acid pickle, and washed with soda or pearl-ash water until it is thoroughly free from dirt or grease, etc., should be connected in five or six clusters loosely, by means of thin silver wire, then annealed and left black. Take a piece of strong silver wire, make a circle a little less in diameter than the top of the black lead crucible (which should hold about a quart,) and make a bail to it, about a foot high, suspend the clusters on the circle. The work is now ready to dip.

Pound the saltpetre and salt fine ; mix them well together by means of the 2 ozs. water, and place the pot on the fire in the forge. When the mixture simmers add the acid, which will immediately commence to boil. Now dip the work and move *gently* up and down for three minutes, then remove it from color, plunge it in a basin of hot water (the basins should be earthenware); plunge again in another basin of hot water, then dip again from half a minute to one minute in the color, then rinse until entirely free from acid. Should any black spots show on the soldered parts, add 2 ozs. hot water, and dip half a minute more, and rinse as before; after this place the work in water sufficient to cover it, and add to the water about an ounce of liquid ammonia; let it remain about ten minutes. Then dip in alcohol and dry in boxwood saw-dust. The pot should be emptied in an earthenware vessel and saved for another time.

BEST ENGLISH FORMULAS

CAREFULLY REVISED AND ADAPTED TO

THE AMERICAN TRADE.

ALLOYS OF ONE OUNCE OR NEARLY, FOR JOBBING.
Dry Colored Gold Alloys.

In all these recipes, unless otherwise expressed, the constituents named will always mean fine gold, fine silver, and refined copper, unless the contrary is stated.

No. 1. 17 k.—Gold 15 dwts.; silver 1 dwt., 10 grs.; copper 4 dwts., 17 grs.

No. 2. 18 k.—Gold 1 oz.; silver 4 dwts., 10 grs.; copper 2 dwts., 5 grs.

No. 3. 18 k.—Gold 15 dwts.; silver 2 dwts., 4 grs.; copper 2 dwts., 19 grs.

No. 4. 18 k —Gold 18 dwts.; silver 2 dwts., 18 grs.; copper 3 dwts., 18 grs.

No. 5. 18 k.—Gold 1 oz., 1 dwt., 6 grs; silver 3 dwt., 10 grs.; copper 4 dwts., 12 grs.

No. 6. 19 k.—Gold 1 oz.; silver 2 dwts., 6 grs.; copper 3 dwts., 12 grs.

No. 7. 20 k.—Gold 1 oz.; silver 2 dwts.; copper 2 dwts., 4 grs.

No. 8. 22 k.—Gold 18 dwts.; silver .12 grs.; copper 1 dwt., 3 grs.

Or, Take English sovereigns, which are 22 k. fine, but they have too'little copper to wear well.

SOLDER FOR ABOVE ALLOYS.

In making gold solder for the foregoing alloys, take of the alloyed gold which you are using 1 dwt.; silver 6 grs. Or, Gold, alloyed as before, 1 dwt.; silver 5 grs.; copper 1 gr.

ALLOY FOR DRY-COLORED RINGS. 17 k.

Gold 1 oz.; silver 4 dwts., 6 grs; copper 4 dwts., 6 grs.

SOLDER FOR THE ABOVE.

Scrap gold 2 oz.; silver 3 dwts.; copper 3 dwts.

OF DRY COLORING THE FOREGOING ALLOYS.

This is done as follows: — Having your work well polished, take of saltpetre, alum, and salt in proportion to the work to be colored; say, for 2 oz. of work, as under, viz.: — Saltpetre 8 oz; alum 4 oz.; salt 4 oz. Procure also a blacklead pot, four or five inches high, or an iron pot cast from a blacklead pot; one or two sizes will be useful. To perform the process of Dry-Coloring, you must have a thin iron bar to stir your " color " when dissolving. Your work cannot be too well polished; it is then cleaned with soda, soap, and hot water, and dried in box sawdust. It must be afterward covered with a thin layer of borax; annealed and boiled out, and again dried in box-sawdust; and finally hung on platinum, or fine silver wire. When the " color" is in the pot, it is placed in the fire on a forge, and blown with bellows; it soon boils up. The heat cannot be too strong. When it assumes a brown-yellow flame, the work is dipped in for two or three seconds, and quenched in hot water diluted with muriatic acid, which removes any " color " that may adhere to the work. This ought to produce the color required; if it does not come, the same process must be followed again; but the work must be well dried before going into the " color," otherwise it will fly

about, the burn or scald from which is very severe. Indeed,
it is recommended to wear an old glove to save the hand.
The color-pot must be emptied immediately upon the forge,
so that it may be ready if required again. In this process
of coloring it is necessary to be very quick, whereas in
Wet-Coloring it takes time. The waste "color" may be
thrown into the sweep, as the gold lost is trifling.

WET COLORED GOLD ALLOYS.

No. 1. 15 k —Gold 1 oz.; silver 3 dwts., 12 grs.; copper 9 dwts.

No. 2. 14 k.—Gold 1 oz. ; silver 4 dwts.; copper 9
dwts., 12 grs.

No. 3. 14 k.—Gold 1 oz.; silver 4 dwts., 12 grs.; copper 10 dwts.

No. 4. 13 k —Gold 1 oz.; silver 4 dwts, 12 grs.; copper 10 dwts., 12 grs.

GREEN GOLD FOR FANCY WORK.

No. 5. 18 k.—Gold 1 oz. ; silver 6 dwts., 16 grs.

GREEN GOLD.

No. 6. 20 k.—Gold 10 dwts.; silver 2 dwts., 2 grs.

GREEN GOLD.

No. 7. 19 k.—Gold 5 dwts.; silver 1 dwt, 12 grs.

RED GOLD, FOR FANCY WORK.

No. 8. 16 k.—Gold 5 dwts.; copper 2 dwts, 12 grs

RED GOLD.

No. 9. 19 k. (20 k so called)—Gold 5 dwts.; copper 1
dwt., 6 grs.

To make gold solder for the foregoing alloys, take of the
alloyed gold you are using, 1 dwt. ; silver 6 grs. Or, 5
grs., of silver and 1 gr. of copper may be used.

ANOTHER SOLDER.

Gold alloyed 1 dwt. ; silver 5 grs. ; pin-brass 1 gr.

This solder is good for repairing, and will not disturb the solder first mentioned.   It will color well.

ALLOY.

No. 10. 15 k.--Gold 1 oz , 18 dwts. ; silver 12 dwts., 12 grs. ; copper 10 dwts.

No. 11. 14 k.—Gold 1 oz ; silver 8 dwts. ; copper 4 dwts.

No. 12. 13 k.—Gold 1 oz. ; silver 6 dwts. ; copper 8 dwts.

No. 13. 13 k.—Gold 1 oz. ; silver 4 dwts., 12 grs. ; copper 10 dwts., 12 grs.   This is usually employed by the London jewelers for their 14 k. work.

VERY FINE COLOR.

No. 14. 16 k.—Gold 1 oz. ; silver 6 dwts.; copper 4 dwts.

GOLD SOLDER FOR THE ABOVE.

Gold scrap 1 oz.; silver 5 dwts.

METHODS OF REDUCING ENGLISH SOVEREIGNS TO LOWER FINENESS.

No. 1. 14 k.—Coins 1 oz.; gold 8 oz.; silver 2 oz.; copper 4 oz., 14 dwts.

No. 2. 14 k.—Coins 1 oz.; gold 2 oz. ; silver 13 dwts. ; copper 1 oz., 11 dwts.

No. 3. 14 k.—Coins 2 oz. ; gold 5 oz. ; silver 1 oz., 9 dwts., 12 grs. ; copper 11 dwts., 12 grs.

No 4. 15 k.—Coins 2 oz.; gold 6 oz. ; silver 1 oz., 14 dwts. ; copper 4 oz., 2 dwts.

No. 5. 15 k.—Coins 2 oz. ; gold 8 oz. ; silver 2 oz., 3 dwts. ; copper 5 oz., 3 dwts.

No. 6. 15 k.—Coins 4 oz ; gold 6 oz. ; silver 2 oz., 2 dwts. ; copper 5 oz., 2 dwts

LONDON METHOD OF WET-COLORING THE FOREGOING ALLOYS.

This is performed in the following manner :—Having annealed your work, and boiled it out so as to get it perfectly clean, take of saltpetre 15·oz., of alum 7 oz. and of salt 7 oz.; pound them all fine, and mix well together ; then provide a black-lead pot about 12 inches high, put your ingredients into it, and dissolve gradually. It must be on no account hurried, for if it burns, the "color" will be spoiled. As the heat increases it will boil up ; the nadd 2 oz. of muriatic acid, when the "color" will sink in the pot. Take a wooden spoon and stir it well, when it will again boil up. Take your work, which you have made clean, and tied in small parcels with platinum or fine silver wire, and immerse it in the "color" for four minutes, keeping it on the move, so that the "color" may act upon all parts alike. At the end of that time take it out and rinse it well in boiling water, which you have ready in a kettle, with pint or quart basins, according to the quantity or size of your work. Next, place your work in the "color" for one minute and a half; take it out and rinse well in fresh hot water. Two fluid oz. of hot water must then be added, when the "color" will sink in the pot, but will rise again ; put in your work for one minute, again rinsing it in fresh hot water, when you will find it begin to brighten. Lastly, put your work in the "color" for half a minute longer, rinsing it for the last time in clean hot water, after which you will find it a beautiful color. This process, by a little attention, never fails.

NOTE.—The mixture of "coloring" should be according to the weight of work. If a small quantity, say 2 oz. the proportions should be :—Saltpetre 8 oz., alum 4 oz, common salt 4 oz., muriatic acid 1 oz. If 5 oz., of work, double the quantities, and so in proportion to the weight; but practice will make perfect.

WET COLORING BY THE GERMAN PROCESS.

Tie up your work in small bunches with fine silver or platinum wire ; then, for 3 oz, of work, take a blackl-ead pot, 6 or 7 inches high, and put it on the fire, for it to get thoroughly dry. As soon as the black-lead pot is quite dry (having previously placed your work in hot water,) put into the pot, of saltpetre 6 oz, and of common salt 3 oz.; stir them well with a wooden spoon, and when thoroughly dried fine and hot, put into it 5 fluid oz. of muriatic acid.

When boiling up, put in your bunch of work, having previously shaken the water from it, and keep it on the move for three minutes, care being taken to keep it well covered all this time.   At the end of this time, take it out and plunge it into a vessel of clean hot water, and finally into a second vessel of the same.   Add then to your "color" in the pot 6 fluid oz. of hot water, and when it boils up again, after being thus diluted, put in your work for one minute longer, and again rinse it as before directed, when it will be found to be a beautiful color.

Too much clean hot water cannot be used for plunging the work in each time through the "color." If the work is hollow-work and bulky, not quite so much as 3 oz. should be put, as it is not so effectually covered in the pot.

In wet-coloring it sometimes happens that the color is rather dead; or it may happen that the "color" burns, which causes the work to look brown; this is a precipitation which may be removed by scratching at the lathe with stale beer or ale, with a fine brass wire brush, similar to the round hair brushes used for polishing.

In coloring, a large stone jar should be provided, into which should be emptied your "color" when done with, for the pot should be washed out each time, so as to be ready when required again.   Into this stone jar should also be emptied the water in which you rinse your work, as it all contains gold to a great extent.

All things connected with the process should be kept clean and free from grease of any kind.

No Iron ought to be near this Wet-Color in the pot, as it is most injurious.

TO COLLECT THE GOLD LOST IN COLORING.

Where there is a large amount of work made and colored, the loss is estimated at 1 dwt. or more per oz.; this in time becomes a serious matter.   To collect that loss the following method is used:—Take one of the basins you use, and put into it a handful of Sulphate of Iron, and pour boiling water upon it to dissolve it.   When dissolved pour it into your stone jar in which you keep your color water; this precipitates the small particles of gold, and must be done each time you color. It should be collected every six months, if the amount of work colored be much, in the following manner :—

With a syphon draw off the water from your jar, but in doing so, be careful not to disturb the sediment which is at the bottom, for it contains the gold. After you have got off what water you can, it must be washed with three or four kettlefulls of boiling water, each kettlefull being done separately, and allowed to cool each time and the water carefully got off; this is to clear the sediment of any acid. It is known to be sufficiently done by touching the water with the finger and tasting it.

When freed from acid put it into an iron pan and dry gradually by the fire. When dried, put it into an iron ladle and make it red hot, stirring it carefully with a tobacco-pipe, care being taken not to spill it. It will turn red in annealing.

Having proceeded thus far, take of the sediment thus prepared 1 oz., of borax pounded fine 15 dwts., of common bottle-glass pounded fine 5 dwts., and of pearlash pounded fine 4 dwts.; mix all well together. Put this into a skittle-pot, which should have a cover, and in placing it in the furnace there should be a small pot reversed for the skittle-pot to stand on. You then lay your fire, which must be lighted at the top, so that the light particles of gold may be carried downward. After the fire is at its hight it is continued for forty minutes, then allowed to burn out, when the metal will be found at the bottom of the pot. This you refine with saltpetre.

Even if jewelers did not wish to collect for themselves, they would find the benefit of taking care of this sediment, and selling it to the refiners.

Too much care cannot be taken in procuring the pure spirits of salts, or muriatic acid.

ALLOYS OF GOLD FOR ENAMELING, ETC.

PALE GOLD FOR ENAMELING, OR LAPPING.

No. 1.—Gold 1 oz.; silver 9 dwts.; copper 2 dwts., 12 grs.

No. 2.—Gold 1 oz.; silver 9 dwts.; copper 3 dwts., 12 grs.

No. 3.—Gold 1 oz.; silver 10 dwts.; copper 3 dwts., 12 grs.

DEEPER COLOR.

No. 4—Gold 1 oz.; silver 1 dwt., 12 grs.; copper 2 dwts., 12 grs.

No. 5.—Gold 1 oz.; silver 9 dwts., 12 grs.; copper 7 dwts., 12 grs.

No. 6.—Gold 1 oz.; silver 14 dwts.; copper 8 dwts.

No. 7.—Gold 2 oz., 5 dwts.; silver 1 oz., 6 dwts.; copper 5 dwts.; pin-brass 5 dwts.

No. 8.—Gold 1 oz.; silver 12 dwts.; copper 6 dwts.

ENAMELING GOLD, FOR TRANSPARENT ENAMELING.

Gold 1 oz.; silver 14 dwts.; copper 6 dwts.

GOLD SOLDER FOR ENAMELED WORK.

Gold 1 oz.; silver 1 oz.; copper 10 dwts.; silver solder 8 dwts., 8 grs.

ANOTHER.

Gold alloyed 1 dwt.; silver 4 grs.

ANOTHER SOLDER.

Gold 12 dwts.; silver 7 dwts., 3 grs.; copper 6 dwts.

PALE GOLD ALLOYS FOR POLISHING.

No. 1.—Gold 1 oz.; silver 8 dwts.; copper 3 dwts., 12 grs.

No. 2.—Gold 1 oz.; silver 1 dwt., 20 grs.; copper 1 dwt., 4 grs.

No. 3.—18 k. pale gold 1 oz.; silver 4 dwts.; copper 2 dwts , 15 grs.

No. 4.—Another.—18 k. gold 1 oz., 12 grs.; silver 3 dwts., 8 grs.; copper 3 dwts., 8 grs.

PALE GOLD SOLDER.

Gold alloyed 1 dwt., 6 grs.; silver 1 dwt.

ALLOYS FOR GOLD PENS.

ALLOY FOR BEST PENS.

Gold 1 oz.; silver 5 dwts.; copper 7 dwts., 18 grs.; spelter, 1 dwt., 6 grs.

SOLDER FOR THE ABOVE.

Gold 12 dwts.; silver 7 dwts., 3 grs.; copper 6 dwts.

ALLOY FOR MEDIUM QUALITY PENS.

Gold 1 oz.; composition 1 oz., 13 dwts.

COMPOSITION No. 1. FOR THE ABOVE

Silver 1 oz., 17 dwts.; copper 5 oz., 15 dwts.; spelter 18 dwts., 20 grs.

SOLDER FOR THE FOREGOING.

Gold 1 oz.; silver 1 oz.; brass 1 oz.

GOLD FOR COMMON PENS.

Gold 1 oz.; silver 2 oz.; copper 1 oz.

SOLDER FOR THE FOREGOING.

Gold 1 oz.; silver 2 oz.; pin brass 1 oz.

BRASS GOLD.

No. 1.—Gold 1 oz.; silver 5 dwts. 6 grs.; copper 3 dwts., 12 grs.; pin brass 18 dwts.

No. 2.—Gold 1 oz.; silver 4 dwts.; copper 4 dwts.; pin brass 16 dwts.

No. 3.—Gold 1 oz.; silver 5 dwts , 12 grs.; copper 3 dwts., 12 grs.; pin brass 19 dwts., 6 grs.

In melting the brass-gold it often happens that the gold, to the naked eye, seems all right, yet when it comes to be flattened at the mill, it is full of air and not fit for use; this may be avoided by having a tobacco-pipe to stir the metal when it is in fusion. The nature of the alloys, and the quantity of borax used as flux, is the cause; but acting on the advice given, and by applying sufficient heat, this may be avoided.

No. 4.—Gold 1 oz.; silver 3 dwts., 21 grs.; copper 9 dwts., 3 grs.; composition 5 dwts., 6 grs.

No. 5.—Gold 15 dwts., 9 grs.; silver 5 dwts., 19 grs.; copper 3 dwts., 21 grs.; composition 15 dwts.

COMPOSITION FOR THE ABOVE.

Copper 1 oz.; spelter 5 dwts.

In making solder for the foregoing alloys, take of the alloyed gold you are using, 1 dwt.; silver 12 grs.

HANDY TABLE OF ALLOYS,

FOR DIFFERENT QUALITIES OF GOLD, FOR JOBBING JEWELERS.

QUALITY.	FINE GOLD.			COMPOSITION.			TOTAL.		
	Oz.	Dwts.	Grs.	Oz.	Dwts.	Grs.	Oz.	Dwts.	Grs.
9 Carat...	0	7	12	0	12	12	1	0	0
12 " ..	0	10	0	0	10	0	1	0	0
15 " ..	0	12	12	0	7	12	1	0	0
18 " ..	0	15	0	0	5	0	1	0	0
22 " ..	0	18	18	0	1	6	1	0	0

COMPOSITION FOR THE ABOVE.

Silver 3 oz., 5 dwts., 12 grs.; copper 8 oz., 12 dwts., 12 grs.; spelter 1 oz., 18 dwts., 6 grs.

ALLOY FOR GOLD CHAINS.

No. 1.—Gold 11 dwts., 6 grs.; silver 2 dwts., 5 grs.; copper 6 dwts., 13 grs.

No. 2.—Gold 1 oz.; silver 9 dwts.; copper 8 dwts.

ALLOY FOR PINS.—10 k.

Gold 1 oz.; silver 5 dwts.; copper 1 oz.; spelter 5 dwts.

LONDON BRIGHT GOLD.—9 k.

Gold 1 oz.; silver 7 dwts.; composition 1 oz., 6 dwts.

GOLD 8 k.

Gold 1 oz.; silver 8 dwts.; composition 1 oz., 12 dwts.

COMPOSITION FOR MAKING 9 K. GOLD ACCORDING TO LONDON PRACTICE AS ABOVE.

Copper, 44 oz.; spelter 8 oz.

GOLD 8 k.

Gold 5 dwts.; silver 3 dwts., 6 grs.; copper 6 dwts., 12 grs.

CALIFORNIA.

Gold 11 oz.; composition 15 oz., 10 dwts.

COMPOSITION FOR CALIFORNIA.

Silver 15 oz., 12 dwts.; copper 67 oz.; spelter 11 oz.

SPELTER ALLOY.

8 k. gold 1 oz., 13 dwts, 6 grs.; silver 1 oz., 12 dwts., 12 grs.; copper 1 oz., 16 dwts., 6 grs.; spelter 4 dwts.
Will stand the aquafortis very well.

TO CLEAN OLD WORK THAT IS TARNISHED.

This is done by heating the articles gently with a blow-pipe, and boiling out in rather strong pickle of muriatic acid; it may be removed by boiling in chloride of lime and water in a pipkin, and touching the work at a lathe with a scratch-brush.

TO REMOVE SOFT-SOLDER FROM WORK TO BE MENDED OR COLORED

Remove what you can by the scraper, or otherwise gently heating it, so that you may shake all off that you can. Place it in spirits of salts for some time. This recipe is useful where hard-soldering is required, whether in colored or bright work.

SILVER ALLOYS.

No. 1.—Silver 11 oz., 2 dwts. ; copper 18 dwts.

No. 2.—Silver 1 oz.; copper 1 dwts., 12 grs.

No. 3.—Silver 1 oz.; copper 5 dwts.

ALLOY FOR PLATING.

Silver 1 oz.; copper 10 dwts.

SILVER SOLDER.

No. 1.—Silver 1 oz.; pin-brass 10 dwts.

No. 2.—Silver 1 oz.; pin-brass 10 dwts.; pure spelter 2 dwts.

In fine silver filigree-work, fine silver is always used for the filigree. The framework is generally made of sterling silver. The solder for such work is as follows :—Silver 4 dwts., 9 grs.; pin-brass 1 dwt.

COPPER SOLDER. FOR PLATING.

Silver 10 dwts. ; copper 10 dwts.

This is a useful solder for plating or soldering silver work ; it never eats as does silver solder.

COMMON SILVER, FOR CHAINS.

Silver 6 oz. ; copper 4 oz.

SOLDER FOR THE ABOVE.

Silver 16 dwts. ; copper 12 grs. ; pin-brass 3 dwts., 12 grs.

SILVER SOLDER, FOR ENAMELING.

Silver 14 dwts.; copper 8 dwts.

COMMON SILVER SOLDER.

Silver 20 oz.; pin-brass 13 oz.; spelter 1 oz.

SOLDER FOR FILLING SEAL RINGS.

Silver 20 oz.; copper 3 oz., 8 dwts.; pin-brass 13 oz.; spelter 1 oz.

QUICK SILVER SOLDER.

Silver 1 oz.; pin brass 10 dwts.; bar tin 2 dwts.

SILVER SOLDER, FOR GOLD PLATING,

Silver 1 oz.; copper 5 dwts.; pin brass 5 dwts.

BISMUTH SOLDER.

Bismuth 12 oz.; lead 15 oz.; tin 21 oz.

IMITATIONS.

IMITATION SILVER.

Silver 1 oz.; nickel 1 oz., 11 dwts.; copper 2 oz., 9 dwts.

No. 2.—Silver 3 oz.; nickel 1 oz ,.11 dwts.; copper 2 ozs., 9 dwts.; spelter 10 dwts.

IMITATION GOLD.

Silver 2 ozs., 5 dwts.; copper 1 oz.; composition (44 oz. copper to 8 oz. spelter,) 1 oz.

The above will keep its color very well, and costs about $1 per. oz.

ENAMELS.

An Enamel is a species of vitreous varnish, colored with metallic oxides, applied in a thin stratum to brightly polished metallic surfaces (copper or gold), on which it is fused by the flame of a lamp urged by the blowpipe, or by the heat of a small furnace.

FRITS; OR WHITE FLUX.

The basis of all enamels is a highly transparent and fusible glass, called Frit, Flux, or Paste, which readily receives a color on the addition of metallic oxides. It may be made by one or other of the following formulæ:

No. 1.—Red lead, 16 parts; calcined borax, 3 parts; powdered flint glass, 12 parts; powdered flints, 4 parts; fuse in a Hessian crucible for 12 hours, then pour it out into water, and reduce it to a powder in a biscuit-ware mortar.

No. 2.—Tin 3 parts; lead 10 parts; mix, calcine in an iron pot at a dull cherry-red heat, and scrape off the oxide as it forms, observing to obtain it quite free from undecomposed metal; then reduce it to fine power by grinding and elutriation In this state it is known among enamelers as Flux, or Calcine. 4 parts of this calcine are next mixed with an equal weight of pure sand or powdered flints, and 1 part of sea salt, or other alkaline matter; the mixture is then partially fused in a Hessian crucible, by which it undergoes semi-vitrification.

No. 3. (Chaptal).—Lead and tin equal parts; calcine as above, and take of the mixed oxides or calcine and ground flints of each, 1 part; pure carbonate of potash, 2 parts; and proceed as before.

No. 4. (Wynn).—Flint glass 3 oz.; red lead 1 oz.; as last.

No. 5. (Wynn)—Red lead 18 parts, borax (not calcined), 11 parts; flint glass 16 parts; as last.

No 6. (Wynn).—Powdered flints 10 parts; nitre and white arsenic, of each, 1 part; as last.

The precise qualities of the products of the above processes depend greatly upon the duration and degree of heat employed. By increasing the quantity of sand, glass or flux, the enamel is rendered more fusible, and the opacity and whiteness is increased by the addition of oxide of tin. The use of borax should be avoided, or it should be used sparingly, as it is apt to make the enamel effloresce and lose color.

BLACK ENAMEL.

No. 1.—Calcined iron (protoxide), 12 parts; oxide of cobalt 1 part; mix, add an equal weight of white flux, and fuse as before.

No. 2. (Clouet).—Pure clay 3 parts; protoxid of iron 1 part. A fine black.

No. 3.—Peroxide of manganese 3 parts; zaffre 1 part; mix and add it, as required, to white flux.

BLUE ENAMEL

No. 1.—White frit or flux, colored with oxide of cobalt.

No. 2 —Sand, red lead and nitre, of each, 10 parts ; flint glass or ground flints, 20 parts; oxide of cobalt 1 part, more or less; depending on the desired depth of color.

BROWN ENAMEL.

No. 1.—Manganese 5 parts; red lead 16 parts; flint powder 8 parts ; as before.

No. 2. (Wynn).—Manganese 9 parts; red lead 34 parts; flint powder 16 parts.

No. 3.—Red lead and calcined iron, of each 1 part; antimony, litharge and sand, of each 2 parts. To be added in any required proportion to white frit, according to the color desired. A little oxide of cobalt or zaffre is frequently added to alter the shade.

GREEN ENAMEL.

No 1.—Flux or frit 2 lb.; black oxide of copper 1 oz.; as before.

No. 2.—As the last, but adding red oxide of iron, ½ dr. Less decisive.

No. 3.—Copper dust and litharge of each 2 oz.; nitre 1 oz.; sand 4 oz.; flux or frit according to color wanted.

No. 4 —From transparent frit, any quantity ; oxide of chormium enough to color. Color superb; it will stand a great heat, in common hands however, it frequently turns on the dead leaf tinge.

No. 5 —Transparent flux 5 oz.; black oxide of copper 20 to 40 grs.; oxide of chromium 2 grs. Resembles the emerald.

No. 6.-- From blue and yellow enamel mixed in the required proportions.

OLIVE ENAMEL.

Blue enamel 2 parts ; black and yellow enamel, of each 1 part. See brown enamel.

ORANGE ENAMEL.

No. 1 —Red lead 12 parts ; red sulphate of iron and oxide of antimony, of each 1 part; flint powder 3 parts; calcine together, powder, and melt with flux, 50 parts.

No. 2. (Wynn).—Red lead 12 parts; oxide of antimony, 4 parts; flint powder 3 parts; red sulphate of iron 1 part; calcine, then add flux 5 parts, to every 2 parts of this mixture.

PURPLE ENAMEL.

No. 1.—Flux or frit, colored with oxide of gold, purple precipitate of cassius, or peroxide of manganese.

No. 2.—Sulphur, nitre, green vitriol, antimony, and oxide of tin, of each 1 lb.; red lead, 60 lbs.; mix fuse, cool, powder, and add rose copper, (red oxide), 19 oz.; zaffre 1 oz.; crocus martis $1\frac{1}{2}$ oz.; borax 3 oz.; and of a compound formed of gold, silver and mercury, 1 lb.; fuse, stirring the melted mass with a copper rod all the time, then place it in crucibles, and submit them to the action of a reverberatory furnace for 24 hours. This is said to be the purple enamel used in the mosaic pictures in St. Peter's at Rome.

RED ENAMEL.

No. 1.—Paste or flux colored with the red oxide or protoxide of copper. Should the color pass into the green or brown from the partial peroxidation of the copper, from the heat being raised too high, the red color may be restored by the addition of any carbonaceous matter, as tallow or charcoal.

No. 2.—By tinging the glass or flux with the oxide or salts of gold, or with the purple precipitate of cassius. These substances produce shades of red, inclining to crimson or purple of the most exquisite hue. The enamel often comes from the fire quite colorless, and afterward receives its rich hue at the lamp.

No. 3. (Wynn).—Sulphate of iron (calcined dark), 1 part; a mixture of 6 parts of flux (No. 5), and 1 of colcothar, 3 parts. Dark red.

No. 4. (Wynn).—Red sulphate of iron 2 parts; flux (No. 1) 6 parts; white lead 3 parts. Light red.

ROSE COLORED ENAMEL.

Purple enamel (or its elements) 3 parts; flux 90 parts; mix and add silver leaf or oxide of silver 1 part, or less.

TRANSPARENT ENAMEL.

The frit or flux described above, without coloring matter.

VIOLET ENAMEL.

No. 1.—Purple enamel 2 parts; red enamel (No. 2,) 3 parts; frit 6 parts.

No. 2.—Saline or alkaline frit or flux, any quantity; peroxide of manganese, enough to color. As the tint depends on the metal being at the maximum of oxidation, contact with oily or carbonaceous substances should be particularly avoided.

WHITE ENAMEL.

No. 1.—Calcine (from 2 parts of tin and 1 part of lead), 1 part; fine crystal glass or frit 2 parts; manganese, a few grains; powder, mix, melt and pour the fused mass into clean water; again powder, and fuse, and repeat the whole process 3 or 4 times, avoiding contamination with smoke, dirt, or oxide of iron   A fine dead white.

No. 2 —Washed diaphoretic antimony 1 part; fine glass (free from lead) 3 parts; mix, and proceed as before. Very fine.

No. 3.—Lead 30 parts; tin 33 parts; calcine as before, then fuse 50 parts of this calcine with an equal weight of flints in powder, and 100 parts of salt of tartar.   A fine dead white enamel.

For white enamel, the articles must be perfectly free from foreign admixture, as this would impart a color. When well managed, either of the above forms will produce a paste that will rival the opal.

YELLOW ENAMEL.

Superior yellow enamels are less easily produced than those of most other colors; they require very little flux, and that mostly of a metallic nature. The following come highly recommended by experienced artists:

No. 1.—From frit or flux, fuse with oxide of lead, and a little red oxide of iron.

No. 2.—Lead, tin ashes, litharge, antimony, and sand of each, 1 oz.; nitre 4 oz.; mix, fuse and powder; and add the product to flux or frit, enough to *reduce* the color.

No. 3.—White oxide of antimony, alum, and sal
ammoniac, of each 1 part; pure carbonate of lead from 1
to 3 parts, (all in powder); mix and expose them to a
heat sufficiently high to decompose the sal ammoniac.
Used as the last. Very bright colored.

No. 4 (Wynn).—Red lead 8 oz.; oxide of antimony and
tin, calcined together, of each 1 oz.; mix and add of flux
(No. 5), 15 oz.; mix well and fuse.

No. 5.—Pure oxide of silver added to the metallic fluxes.
The salts of silver are also used, but are are more difficult
to manage. If a thin film of oxide of silver be spread over
the surface of the enamel to be colored, exposed to a
moderate heat, then withdrawn, and the film of reduced
silver on the surface removed, the part under will be found
tinged of a fine yellow. (Clouet.)

AN IMPORTANT WANT SUPPLIED.

THERE has long been an urgent want of a book of designs, suitable for Car, Coach, Fresco and other Painters, and Jewelers, Lithographers, Engravers, &c , which should meet the varied wants of these professions, and be furnished at a moderate price. Most books of ornamentation seem designed more for display than to afford assistance. Desirous of furnishing a book of fresh practical designs of beauty and utility, we secured the aid of Mr. J. H. Loudolphe, an eminent designer and practical painter, and now offer a

BOOK OF SCROLLS AND ORNAMENTS

FOR ONE DOLLAR PER COPY.

Though we have desired to make this work moderate in price, our *first* aim has been to make it good. Mr. Loudolphe is a well-known practical man, whose work in the shop speaks for itself He has endeavored, in preparing our designs, to give just what would be most useful and valuable in actual use, rather than to make a fine looking book. We believe examination and trial will prove them well adapted to the requirements of the trade, and to be satisfactory in every respect. It will be observed that each plate contains a large variety of designs, duplication being avoided, and by varying the combinations, as shown in several of the designs, a multitude of effective and beautiful figures may be devised.

Besides many new designs, this work contains the principal ones given by Mr. Loudolphe in a former work, which was published at *four dollars*, and was regarded by experts as well worth the price. With the additional matter herewith given, we have no fears in presenting our book. as one of the best as well as by far the cheapest work of the kind yet published.

THE AMERICAN BOOKSELLER'S GUIDE, a cautious critic and the recognized authority in the book trade, says :

Messrs. Jesse Haney & Co. have issued a *Book of Scrolls and Ornaments* which will add to the very favorable reputation their Trade Manuals and Handbooks have given them. While the price, one dollar, is insignificant compared with the usual cost of books of ornamentation, this book for all practical purposes seems to be actually their superior.

For sale by all booksellers, or mailed post-paid on receipt of price, One Dollar, by

JESSE HANEY & COMPANY, Publishers,

No. 119 Nassau Street, New York.

Good Books for Self-Improvement.

SELF CURE of STAMMERING and STUTTERING.

Gives a clear and full explanation of the most successful modes of treatment, and enables the stammerer to cure himself without surgical operation or machinery, and without *cost*. **25** cents.

Self-Cure of Debility, Consumption, Dyspepsia, Nervous Diseases, &c.

This book is issued in response to an urgent demand. It tells the real nature of many things which have been grossly misrepresented by unprincipled medical pretenders, enabling the patient himself to ascertain his real condition, to distinguish between the important and the unimportant "symptoms," and to escape the extortions of quacks, and to cure himself by simple means, within reach of all without any expense. The need of a reliable book of this kind, while lying and vulgar pamphlets are scattered in millions by quacks, is evident. Our book is simple in language, explicit in all directions, and founded on the very soundest medical science. The means of treatment are always safe, avoiding all the dangers of empirical tampering and proprietary "nostrums," and are the most approved and successful of the regular faculty. They are the surest, safest, speediest, simplest and most thorough means of cure that are known. **75** cents.

RAPID RECKONING.

A system of performing arithmetical calculations with almost instantaneous quickness. This system was the key to the wonderful performances of the "Lightning Calculator," whose exhibitions were the marvel of thousands. He sold the secret at $1 per copy. Our book is much enlarged, with many interesting additions. Any one can learn and practice. Valuable to bookkeepers, teachers, students and all business men. **25** cents.

IMPROVEMENT OF MEMORY.

Shows how to make a bad memory good and a good memory better; the system enabling all to strengthen their memories and often display a power which is surprising. **15** cents.

EMPLOYMENT SEEKERS' GUIDE.

Designed to present the advantages and disadvantages of various trades and professions, advice on investing money, starting in business, obtaining employment, qualifications necessary for different purposes, deceptive undertakings, comparative value of different schemes for money making, and much useful and interesting matter, especially valuable to the young and inexperienced, enabling them to make best use of their abilities and avoid snares of sharpers and quicksands of business. **25** cents. In press.

THE TAXIDERMIST'S MANUAL.

HANEY'S PAINTER'S MANUAL.

A plain and concise guide for practical painters, and aims to give such information as will be useful to the general profession, embracing the best methods and latest improvements in painting, graining, varnishing, polishing, staining, gilding, glazing, silvering, Grecian oil-painting, Chinese and Oriental painting, etc. Also principles of glass staining, harmony and contrast of colors, with philosophy, theories and practices of color, etc. Includes also Practical Paper Hanging. 50 cts.

Extract from Author's Preface.

"It is not proposed in the following pages to compile a work of 'valuable recipes,' which, if followed, would lead the learner into vague uncertainties instead of giving him any light on the subject. Works on decorative art are not generally written by practical men, and consequently are of little practical utility. But this PAINTER'S MANUAL, it is hoped, will be found to contain the very best methods of practice in all that pertains to general painting, which methods are given in as plain and concise a manner as possible. It is proposed also, not to give correct instructions in the art, but, which is of quite as much importance, instruct the painter how to preserve his health, by preventing the deleterious effects of their poisonous colors. In describing work and preparation of colors, great brevity will be used; and the matter is as extensively classified as possible, the object being to make the work useful to learners. Such a book is much needed in this country, for there is not in the country any work of the kind published which is of any practical use to the novice."

What Practical Men Say:

The following are but samples of many approving words from purchasers and users of our Painter's Manual:

"I consider the work invaluable and indispensable to the person engaged in painting, &c., and write from an experience of more than thirty years."—JOHN SALISBURY, Newport, R. I.

"I have one of your books, the Painter's Manual, which I find to contain much valuable information."—S. H. WASHBURN, Vergennes, Vermont.

"I like your Painter's Manual very much. I think that it is the most information for the money that I ever saw."—THOMAS E. WHITNEY, Camden, Ind.

Price, Fifty Cents.

HANEY'S ART OF TRAINING ANIMALS.

This book is a complete guide, the only one fully and specially treating the subject, and *gives more information* about the training of animals *in single chapters* than other *entire books.* Has the most approved methods of the most celebrated and successful trainers, thoroughly initiating the reader into all the secrets of the profession, exposing various bogus "charms," &c., sold to the credulous at high prices, and telling, in fact, *everything* connected with the art of breaking, taming, and training all animals. Besides containing a vast amount of information which will be of real interest and value to farmers and others, it is full of attraction for boys. It not only explains how all the marvelous feats displayed by trained animals at public exhibitions are taught, but shows how many amusing and surprising tricks may be taught by any boy to dogs, ponies or other pets. One gentleman writes us that his boys have organized quite an interesting amateur circus with their pet animals, who have been taught many of the best tricks by following its instructions, and he proposes getting them a little tent.

"Horses firing off pistols, answering questions by nodding or shaking their heads, dancing dogs and bears, performing canary birds and fleas, and the like, are 'some pumpkins,' but how about those wonderful dogs who play dominoes; select from a heap any article therein they are ordered to, and give it to any person named; dogs who spell words by selecting lettered cards, or answer questions, tell your age or your fortune by the same means? Or the monkeys who enact little dramas, personating the characters in a manner to shame many of their human compeers? Or seals who play the hand-organ? Fortunately for the excited juvenile community, a certain Mr. Haney has come to the rescue with a full exposition of the Art of Training Animals, explaining these and hundreds of other feats, to the infinite joy of every boy who can now convert his own pets into a circus troupe at a cost about equal to a single admission to the 'big tent.'"—*N. Y. Evening Express.*

"There is scarcely an animal which has escaped our author's clutches, and he has certainly presented a vast amount of interesting information touching their character and tuition. Not only are the ordinary feats of the circus explained, but the most intricate tricks exhibited by some few renowned 'stars' among animal performers."—*Turf, Field, and Farm.*

"The performances of trained animals have always been painful rather than interesting to us, from the thought of the amount of suffering necessary to bring it about. The author of this book, however, tells us how to train or pet dogs, cats, horses etc., to very wonderful feats at only the expense of a little patience and skill."—*Little Corporal, Chicago.*

"Even those who do not seek it for its information will find it agreeable to read."—*Providence Press.*

"A large variety of information, truly, to be embodied in a single book at so small a price."—*New England Farmer.*

"The raising and training of pets is a pleasurable occupation, and one that we would like to see encouraged among our farmers' boys."—*Prairie Farmer.*

"Mingles with its clear directions a number of pleasant incidental facts, pleasantly told."—*N. Y. Day Book.*

"Furnishes very entertaining reading."—*Phila Daily Ledger.*

"Will entertain both old and young."—*Advance.*

"We have to thank Mr. Haney for many facts regarding animals beyond the mere trainer's province, which it is interesting to know."—*Boston Am. Union.*

210 Pages. 60 Illustrations. Paper Covers 50 cts.; Boards, 75 cts.; Cloth $1.

For sale by booksellers generally, or sent by mail, post-paid, on receipt of price.